Burrswood - Focus of Healing

By the same author:

WITH LOVE TO THE CHURCH

THE END OF OUR EXPLORING

CONTEMPLATING NOW

TRAVELLING IN

PURITAN'S PROGRESS

Monica Furlong

Burrswood - Focus of Healing

HODDER AND STOUGHTON
LONDON SYDNEY AUCKLAND TORONTO

Printed in Great Britain for Hodder and Stoughton Limited, Mill Road, Dunton Green, Sevenoaks, Kent by Tonbridge Printers Limited, Peach Hall Works, Tonbridge, Kent.

Contents

Foreword

I FIRST CAME to Burrswood at the invitation of one of the staff, who was a personal friend. We had visited the opera at Glyndebourne together and she had suggested that I might like to come back with her and spend the night at Burrswood and meet Dr. Aubert and one or two others the next day. We arrived tired and late at night and she showed me to one of the rooms in the nursing home and left me. It was a pretty room, furnished with imagination and love, with a pleasing flower painting on the wall. I was surprised and touched to notice that someone had put a hot-water bottle in the bed. In a moment or two there was a tap on the door and a nurse appeared, introduced herself (as Burrswood nurses, I later discovered, invariably do on their first appearance) and asked if I would like a drink . . . tea, Ovaltine, etc. I felt slightly guilty, in my rude health, at taking up the time of nursing home staff in making me drinks, but I *did* want a drink (I was chilly after the drive) and so gratefully accepted.

I woke up next morning feeling that I was more tired than I had let myself know (something I have often discovered since when staying at Burrswood) and grateful that I did not have to get up in a hurry. When I did get up I was surprised by the width and beauty of the view (my room overlooked the terrace and gardens) and later I walked round the gardens with my friend. Knowing how desperately sick some of the Burrswood patients were I was obscurely surprised at the cheerfulness of the place. My friend introduced me to one or two of the staff and to patients and I liked the quiet friendliness. Later I lunched with Dr. Aubert and was impressed at what he said about the need for co-operation between religion and medicine. It seemed surprising to hear a doctor talking about the importance of belief in sick people, and about the need to treat people as 'whole people', more surprising perhaps then (six years ago) than it would be now.

On the way back to the station my friend said she wondered if I would ever want to write a book about Burrswood. Although I had liked the place, I felt no particular enthusiasm for the task and said so. Spiritual healing seemed to be a subject fraught with difficulties and dangers, and particularly unsuited to someone of my own rather sceptical nature. I disliked the gushing enthusiasms this subject often aroused, the emphasis on 'miracle' (as if all life is not a perpetual miracle), the appeal to human gullibility.

A good many years before, I had been sent, as a journalist, to a meeting in the Albert Hall in which a well-known healer was holding sessions. The opening prayer and hymn were perfunctory. What the audience had come to see was the moment when perhaps half a dozen terribly deformed and crippled people would be helped on to the stage and the healer would cure them. Only the first half dozen could be healed (rather like the Pool of Bethesda) and throughout the hymn the steep stairs of the Albert Hall were covered with sick people literally crawling on their hands and knees, desperately hoping to be among the tiny handful chosen, watched with fascinated curiosity by the audience. It was a horrifying sight and it gave me a bias towards orthodox medicine impossible to shake off.

I did not, of course, class Burrswood with that sort of healing, yet I did fear some sort of short cut, an attempt to make healing simple, when it is, in fact, a complex process.

Another uncertainty for me was the figure of Dorothy Kerin who then, and now, was central to Burrswood's whole understanding of healing. I had heard her called the 'Anglican saint' and since what I find lovable in human beings is not saintliness but their occasional fleeting awareness of their frailty I wondered if I should warm to her. I felt that some existing books about her annihilated her by uncritical admiration, failing to wonder about crucial questions, tactfully passing over alarming eccentricities, yet somehow missing, as the biographers of Bernadette of Lourdes had also wilfully missed, the basic shrewdness, crudeness, tartness (it is difficult to find an apt word) which lies at the core of all human greatness, and supremely, in my opinion, in the central figure of the New Testament. Dorothy Kerin had tended, to those who had not met her, to come over as a 'lady', and Burrswood as an institution that appealed to the 'well-to-do', and neither ladies, nor the well-to-do seemed nowadays to be relevant to the human condition.

Finally, there was a personal inhibition, only half realised by me at the time. Having enjoyed almost perfect physical health, I knew little of physical illness, and, childbirth and toothache apart, little of physical pain. What little I did know frightened me, and I did not seek to extend my knowledge. As a small child I had been taken to see my father in hospital when he was recovering from an operation. Already frightened and bewildered at seeing my father ill I had had the misfortune to witness the patient in the next bed having a heart attack, and for months and years afterwards the hospital was a source of nightmares to me. I could never understand people's enthusiasm for talking about sickness and operations, nor their interest in hospitals, and this distaste had persisted into adult life so that I continued to shrink from discussion of illness.

Four years later I was approached officially by the Warden of Burrswood and asked whether I would be prepared to write a book about the place and its work. I was surprised to find how much my own thinking had changed since the subject was last raised. It was partly that there had been a huge increase in general interest in the subject of healing. All kinds of people, inside and outside the churches, and even within the medical profession, had begun to take an interest in the spiritual aspects of healing. There was the usual crop of frauds and cranks, and, perhaps no less harmful, those who are full of enthusiasm and sincerity but who have no sense of human history and experience, no capacity to learn by past mistakes and who dabble in matters far beyond their understanding. None of these charges could be levelled against Burrswood. In every stage of its history, it had taken full advantage of religious and medical experience and tradition; it had, and has, a sort of sturdy commonsense. I began to think that amid the chaos of new ideas on the subject of healing, it might be a kind of steady rock to whom those in bewilderment amidst the terrible fears of sickness and death might turn. At least Burrswood had years of painstaking effort and painful experience behind it, facts which could count for a great deal.

If the world itself had changed in the preceding four years then so had I. A death in my immediate family, acute sickness in a friend, the constant confrontation of agony in the world about one which no seeing person can deny, had made me want to return to the subject of suffering and healing, and think more deeply about it. These experiences began to uncover the old repression of my childhood and seeing illness at first hand made me feel that far from being disgusting it held the clues to much that I needed to know and to learn.

In this mood I travelled down to Burrswood and met Dorothy Arnold and Edward Aubert. I was still doubtful that I could write anything that the Burrswood community would feel did justice to their history and beliefs, and guessing that our ideas were probably poles apart I plunged into the conversation with Edward Aubert by saying "I don't like miracles!" (meaning by this instantaneous healing). The speed and force of Dr. Aubert's reply knocked me off balance.

"Neither do I!" he said. As we talked I felt myself in the presence of a man of great width of perception, ready to ask questions about anything and everything, quiet, non-assertive, yet very much 'there'.

I touched upon my second fear, that I should be forced to subscribe to what I felt was in danger of becoming a 'Dorothy Kerin cult'. I was interested in Miss Kerin as a deeply fascinating and unusual human being, but not as someone beyond all error or criticism. Dr. Aubert talked for a while of his memories of 'Dorothy', of the uncanniness of her vision, of her gaiety 'there was nobody like her at a party', of her rebelliousness as a patient, and finally said in a hurt voice, obviously remembering some past contretemps 'And she could be unfair!' At once I caught a picture of a believable, rounded human being, and felt that that difficulty was removed.

I also, rather shyly, mentioned my buried terrors of illness. Dr. Aubert seemed to find this not at all surprising and in fact confessed, as I have heard other doctors do, that the overcoming of a similar fear had played a part in his own vocation.

I agreed to do the book. Over a period of many months I made a number of visits to Burrswood and got to know it much better. I interviewed staff, talked to patients, and families of patients, went to healing services, wandered about the grounds, ate and slept Burrswood. On one visit I was mildly ill, and discovered what it was like to be looked after in bed there. I talked at length to Dr. Aubert and Dr. Cuming about my impressions. At the same time I tried to set what I saw against the background of a sceptical world, scientifically sophisticated but spiritually naïve, knowing that, as twentieth century people I, and my readers, were inescapably part of that world. I also went to Lourdes, curious to see how the same problems of sickness and death were handled in a Roman Catholic and Continental setting, and was struck by curious resemblances between Dorothy Kerin and Bernadette Soubirous.

In the following pages I have explored most of these themes at length but before doing so I should like to make a general observation or two about my visits. I saw no miracle (in the generally accepted sense of the word) because I sought none. What I did see was a mother who, together with her husband and children, had been carried through the death of a beloved son from leukaemia. I saw a young woman with the courage to face death from incurable cancer. I saw a blind man whose visits to Burrswood made a frustrating and difficult life endurable. I saw a woman able to carry on with a hellish marriage for the same reason. I do not know whether most people regard such things as miracles, though they seem that way to me, but I do know that they made me feel a bit as John the Baptist must have felt when he heard the testimony of Christ's disciples. 'The blind see, the lame walk, the lepers are cleansed, the deaf hear, the dead are raised, to the poor the gospel is preached.' There is an authenticity about giving hope to other human beings because, if it is to be of lasting value and not merely the prelude to an even greater bitterness, it must be the fruit of love, immense patience, and, however widely one interprets the word, of prayer.

The love of the Burrswood staff, and their capacity to 'affirm' those who come there, is immediately striking. Having known a number of communities I was impressed by their ability to love not only those who arrive needing help, but even (a much more difficult task) one another. To love those you live with and cannot escape from involves a real ability to live with 'badness' — one's own and other people's — and it is this maturity perhaps which gives Burrswood its air of quiet and cheerful authority. The Devil is, as it were, given his rightful place, which makes it impossible for him to take over by stealth.

So this book is about Burrswood, but it is not only about Burrswood. Everyone cannot go there (it would be ruined if they did), some wouldn't like it, and it is not even necessarily the pattern everyone should follow. I have come to see it as what Christians call a 'sign', a sort of light-house which may prevent the rest of us, bound on our own hazardous journeys, from being wrecked on the rocks. There is room for a great deal of new thinking about healing, a great deal of experiment with therapeutic communities, and for a whole new understanding of what belief or lack of it has to do with a man's physical or mental healing. If Burrswood's methods, successes, or even their mistakes, can be used to heal the sick or comfort the sorrowing or the dying who have never heard of Burrswood or Dorothy Kerin, I fancy Burrswood would be well pleased.

Finally, there must be a word about Dr. Aubert. I learned of his sudden death when I had completed my researches and was in the throes of writing the book, and it seemed impossible to believe that I should never again meet him in the corridors of Burrswood, (always with time for a smile and chat), never have supper again with him and Deirdre in St. Luke's, never see the twinkle in his eye when I put a question meant to floor him, above all never have a chance to show him the manuscript in which he had shown so much interest. These are selfish considerations — his loss to Burrswood and his patients and family is infinitely greater than mine — but it is a measure of the closeness and love of the Burrswood community, that even a comparative stranger should feel as if she had lost a member of her own family. Because of his interest, and his hope that I should succeed in presenting Burrswood in credible form to a wider public (whether or not I have actually succeeded), it seems right to dedicate the book to him.

Introduction

Burrswood exists because of a hard and terrible fact about human existence; it is that man suffers. He suffers first and foremost because he lives throughout his life in the shadow of his approaching death. He may live seventy, eighty or ninety years, or, more tragically he may die in youth or at the height of his mental and physical powers, but the consciousness of death is never far from him. He watches it in his family and friends, he sees daily evidence of it in the world about him.

He suffers too in a myriad of other ways: sudden epidemics of illness which may attack a community, strange isolated incidents of illness, apparently inexplicable, illnesses induced by his own bad habits and folly, or that of others, illnesses visited upon him as a result of heredity or stress or accident. However much man may talk of progress, or rejoices in the triumphs of technology or medicine, he cannot really escape from the knowledge of his own desperate vulnerability and the vulnerability of all those whom he loves. A wife, husband, child, friend, is a kind of hostage to fortune, and many of us suffer more in the sufferings of those we love than in the bearing of our own misfortunes.

There seems no obvious reason that men and women should not be pessimists, chronically depressed in a harsh world, continually conscious of hostile fate, yet this is by no means frequently the case. Side by side with fear, there is in mankind a cheerfulness, a bubbling joy, a readiness to accept the happiness which life brings as well as the sorrows and a kind of obstinate hope. Even in his bad moments, man usually thinks it is worth going on, he believes that, round the corner at least, there may be some wholeness, some healing, as yet unimaginable. Perhaps he believes it because, in minor ways, he has watched healing processes at work in his own body again and again; the cut knee of his childhood which grew a scab and finally revealed new skin, the attack of measles which gave way to health. He knows that things can get better.

Or he knows it at greater depth because there is a sort of pattern that runs through the core of human experience, and perhaps through the universe itself, a pattern given overt expression in the Christian religion — the pattern of death and resurrection. Death is the condition of life, suffering yields to joy, the agony of conflict is followed by peace.

This kind of belief does not answer the agonised question of those who suffer — 'Why me?' — nor does it settle our endless puzzlement about why, if God loves us, he allows such agony to exist or to continue, but it does create a new vision in those who suffer, which in turn creates a new patience and a new joy. 'Christianity' wrote Simone Weil 'does not offer a supernatural remedy for suffering, but it does suggest a supernatural use for it.' If we suffer with faith, however imperfect or partial, we make a strange discovery — that we are part of one human body, the body which died, not only on Calvary, but which dies and is resurrected daily in the children of God who surround us. Our suffering is part of the tragedy of mankind, but it is also part of its redemption. We may find 'the problem of pain' intractable, yet by living, even in pain, we can find the trust and the joy and the sense of unity which make life rich.

It is the perception of a pattern which makes illness bearable, the perception that there is meaning in the world with which we can, if we will, co-operate. The sublime function of religion has been to point men back again and again to that meaning just when they had lost sight of it. Suffering has been the friend of religion in that, in itself, it often forces us away from trivialities towards the mysteries from which we draw our real nourishment. As one of the Hasidic rabbis put it: 'When a man suffers, he ought not to say: "That's bad! That's bad!" Nothing that God imposes on man is bad. But it is all right to say:

"That's bitter!" For among medicines there are some that are made with bitter herbs.'

Yet there is at the same time, a sense of wrongness, a sense that 'it should not be' about suffering, that has given a powerful direction to man's energies. We want to see wounds healed, crippled limbs made straight, illnesses cured, pain reduced or removed. Vast human resources have been deployed to cure or diminish the miseries of mankind, and in our own time, this has yielded remarkable success. Our skill in using drugs, anaesthetics and mechanical aids such as kidney machines has transformed the picture in many illnesses. Yet in some strange way the sum total of illness and suffering seems to remain about the same, and the goal of wholeness and healing for all to have moved no nearer. Apart from the illnesses which as yet do not yield to treatment, mankind seems to be uncovering, almost inventing, new *malaises* which ensure that his cup of suffering remains as full as ever. There is, at the root of man's soul, a 'dis-ease' which robbed of one form of expression finds another. At the same time, some of man's old wisdom and his old perception of meaning, particularly in regard to death and pain, has got thrown overboard in the optimistic phase of man's voyage, making him in many ways more helpless than his ancestors. They knew, as we find difficulty in remembering, that frailty and death are man's natural condition.

It is, therefore, of little use to multiply 'treatments' that do not look beyond the illness to the fundamental disquiet of mankind. If medicine acts in this way, then, Canute-like, it is going to be gradually submerged in the rising tide of illness (and there is some evidence that this is exactly what is happening). Equally, it is useless to begin at the other end, and treat all illness as spiritual catastrophe. Pain and illness require their own, very specific remedies, which relieve the symptoms, if not the cause. What seems to be needed is a kind of double approach to illness, the doctor recognising, however dimly, the spiritual suffering which lies at the core of much, if not all, illness, the priest respecting the bodily working out of the processes of redemption. Only a close co-operation between doctor and priest or minister, between medicine and religion, would seem to do justice to the astonishing complexity of sickness.

It is this co-operation of which Burrswood is the supreme example. Its Warden is both doctor and priest, it has the constant services of skilled doctors and priests, and a highly trained nursing staff. People who come to it receive orthodox medical treatment, yet have ample opportunity also to talk about their non-medical problems. The hope of healing and of wholeness is evident in everything that happens to patients at Burrswood, yet there is also an understanding of the kind of life which may emerge through the death of hope. There is a real ability to help patients, and their families, to face death itself. "We don't tell lies here!"

For practising Christians there is, in all this, a question more nagging than 'the problem of pain' or the question of how modern illness should be treated in modern times. Of the utmost importance to the Christian faith are the written records of Jesus' life upon earth, the gospels, and these describe case after case of extreme forms of illness or disability — leprosy, epilepsy, paralysis, palsy, blindness, deafness, psychosis, haemorrhage, deformity — which were instantaneously — miraculously healed by the touch or presence of Jesus. These healings, which Christians once confidently offered to agnostics as proof of the divinity of Jesus, have in modern times become almost an embarrassment.

The scientific mood of the nineteenth and twentieth century made miracles harder and harder to swallow and I remember as a child at school an apologetic teacher suggesting to us that the illnesses Jesus cured were all hysterical in origin. If this seemed a little difficult to believe, as in the case of, for instance, congenital deformity, she fell back on the unscholarly temper of the evangelists, their tendency to exaggerate in a good cause.

A different approach to the problem was to point to the uniqueness of Jesus. If Jesus was 'whole man' in the way Christians have believed, then who could know what impact 'wholeness' might have upon a person sick in body or mind. We had all known or heard of, doctors and nurses whose presence simply made the patient 'feel better' — Florence Nightingale is a notable example of someone whose presence, it was widely attested, made a difference to the attitude, and so to the prognosis, of the sick. Imagine a healer who had that capacity to a far greater degree, and it did not seem utterly improbable that his influence might produce dramatic healing.

But what of his disciples? The *Acts of the Apostles* records Peter, James, and other disciples, performing miracles on the sick as if that were the most natural thing in the world, and the gospels record the clear expectation that those who are 'in touch' with Jesus will equally be able to perform his healing role.

> I tell you most solemnly,
> whoever believes in me
> will perform the same works as I do myself,
> he will perform even greater works. John 14, 12.

For a few centuries after the death of Jesus the phenomenon of healing appears to have continued along with other phenomena such as speaking with tongues. The Desert Fathers of 4th century Alexandria could heal the sick, raise the dead, listen, as Jesus and his disciples had done, to the stumbling confessions of those who had lost their way and give counsel. Just as interesting, they were famous for being able to live alongside animals without fear or hurt — they made friends of the jackals and lions that inhabited their lonely landscape, and sometimes shared food and living quarters with them; a different sort of miracle.

But gradually, perhaps with the institutionalising of Christianity, the expectation of Christians that they would be able to heal one another died out. It survived only in odd pockets of Christian life, and perhaps as a wistful hope in the hearts of all Christians. Holy people, saints, were associated with miraculous healing — it came to be an important part of the evidence required for the canonisation of a saint. Even in death saints' bodies or bones were thought to have healing power; the sick and troubled travelled miles to the shrines where saints, or parts of saints, were buried. Or the place where a saint had lived became endowed with healing. Wells, in particular, seemed to carry this transferred healing power, together with fountains and springs. Among others the spring at Lourdes, which Bernadette had found under the direction of 'the Lady', became associated with some remarkable cures.

If places where saints had lived, or their own dead bodies, became agents of healing because of their association with living holiness, so the saints themselves were potent healing agents, they themselves would have felt, because of a particular kind of association with, or incorporation in, the person of Christ. Relics of the life of Jesus upon earth — pieces of the True Cross, etc. — were themselves thought in medieval times to have healing powers like the bones of the saints. The saints themselves were a relic, and more than a relic, of that brief, extraordinary life upon earth. In them Jesus lived on, and in them his special powers continued to be accessible to mankind.

There is no doubt, of course that the whole phenomenon of miracles became the vehicle for the crudest kinds of exploitation. In medieval times relics were a profitable industry, and human gullibility, and the pitiful longing of the sick and the socially deprived for help and healing were shamelessly exploited. But contempt for that kind of cruelty and folly perhaps tended to obscure the fact that miracles did occur, and since miracles seemed to belong to the gullible and priest-dominated world of medieval Catholicism, the Protestants, (in some ways the precursors of science), with their rational, methodical temperament, tended to throw miracles overboard with much else in Catholicism that they regarded as naïve and superstitious.

In any case the vast majority of Christians, Catholic or Protestant, had long ago ceased to expect to be able to perform miracles or to have miracles performed for their benefit. The growing preoccupation of men was not to be able to conjure, influence, or propitiate, the mysterious, and largely unknowable power that lay behind the universe, but rather to be able to control the environment, mechanically, technically, in such a way as to make life better, at least in a material sense.

It is only in recent years that we have begun to note the losses, as well as the tremendous gains, of that changed response to the world. Of course, the giant strides man took not only in the production of wealth and the raising of living standards of the depressed and deprived but also in the relief of pain and the control of disease by advanced surgery and sophisticated use of drugs have shown this preoccupation to be of immeasurable value. It is because of this that it has taken us many years to admit that there are losses as well as gains in the conscious domination of our environment. We have lost much of the sense of oneness with nature which belonged to more primitive men, and with it the capacity to listen to the non-rational voices within us which may give us precious guidance. In our fear of superstition and gullibility we have lost confidence in that inner world of numinosity, of awe, of religious feeling, which meant so much to our forebears, and with it the expectation that healing may come upon us in a form not immediately explicable in terms of drugs or surgery.

Yet the effort to exclude the irrational has had the paradoxical effect predicted by Jung — that the irrational has tended to take us over. Ecstasy, charisma, the non-rational outpouring of the Spirit, has suddenly begun to attract people as it has not done, at least in England, for several hundred years. Within and without the Christian Church there is a great and growing interest in non-rational phenomena. Speaking with tongues, which only twenty years ago was regarded as an oddity that was gone for ever, is no longer rare.

And since sickness is one of the most intractable and inescapable of all human problems, the new movement has been active in this area, praying over the sick, laying hands on them, interceding for them. Faith-healers, that is to say those who set out to cure by non-rational methods, have become much more numerous. Some of them are frauds and quacks, others undoubtedly do heal people of sicknesses in ways for which we can find no rational explanation.

By no means all of these are Christian, nor do they necessarily hold beliefs with which Christians would agree. It looks as if 'the gift of healing' is some special quality within the personality of the healer, like a gift for music, which works quite independently of belief.

Where do Dorothy Kerin and Burrswood fit into this picture? Dorothy Kerin believed in a 'non-rational' healing because she had herself experienced such a healing at the beginning of her adult life, and she was to witness similar healings in her presence again and again throughout her life. She had the gift of healing, but for her it was associated solely with the person of Christ. It was, in her view, Christ who healed. She was only 'the instrument' or 'bit of pipe'. She was a Christian, within the Anglo-Catholic tradition of Christianity, and needed to make sense of her experiences within that tradition, but obviously her convictions went far beyond conventional devotion. She had an almost constant awareness of the presence of Christ, an awareness which she had known first in childhood; if one wanted to express it in the language of Jungian psychology one might say that the archetype of Christ was reanimated in her.

Despite the force of her belief in the non-rational, however, she believed firmly in balancing it with the rational, and this was perhaps one of the greatest things about her. She believed in medicine, medicine practised under the best possible conditions, sustained by the most competent conventional nursing. From the days at Ealing when she first began to care for the sick, she saw that some people would be helped by conventional medicine, some by 'Divine healing', as she called it, but that the two were inseparable, different aspects of the same outworking of the creative Spirit.

At a time when few people, even among practising Christians, believed in non-rational methods of healing, and many were prepared to dismiss Dorothy Kerin as a crank, she was working away, like the rare pioneer that she was, at a way of caring for the sick that used *all* resources for the patient's benefit. On this strong base she established Burrswood — a place where regular, conventional medicine was daily practised, a place where patients were given excellent physical care, a place where patients could talk and be listened to, a place where prayer was regarded as important, a place where the 'laying-on of hands' was available to those who wanted it, a place where miracles sometimes occurred, but where, in any case, people 'got well', a place where it was possible to accept and prepare for death. It was, and it still is, far ahead of its time.

PART ONE

Dorothy Kerin

I

DOROTHY KERIN WAS born on November 28th, 1889, at Walworth, the second of five children, and spent much of her childhood at a house at Herne Hill still in existence — 204 Milkwood Road. Her father was a businessman. When she was twelve her father died and it is possible that this sudden shock just at the onset of puberty affected her health. Her health became very poor and, when she was fifteen, she was seriously affected by catching diphtheria. From this time on she became more or less a permanent invalid, and in time tuberculosis was diagnosed. She was confined to bed. Thus illness robbed her of some of the most precious years of adolescence, years in which the normal girl is preoccupied with friendships, particularly with boys, in which she takes her first independent steps in the world, and in which she completes her education and finds a job.

By the end of 1911, when Dorothy Kerin was twenty-two, her illness had taken a turn for the worse, and she was near to death with advanced tuberculosis and diabetes. She was unconscious for long periods, and when conscious, was suffering great pain from the pressure on her emaciated body as she lay in bed. Her physician had warned her mother that there was no hope of recovery.

In February, however, there was a miraculous intervention, watched by a group of friends and neighbours who had come in to sit with the family in their daughter's last hours. Suddenly the unconscious girl sat up and said "Do you not hear? I am well, I must get up and walk". And the girl did get up and walk, though those in the room tried to dissuade her, presumably thinking she was in delirium. An account written at the time describes Dorothy Kerin going out of the room in search of her stepfather who was not present, finding him and kissing him. She then demanded food — substantial food and not invalid diet — and to the amazement of the company ate cold beef and pickles. Finally she fell into a sound sleep and slept till morning, when her doctor was sent for. To his amazement he found her not only up, but well. Her body had recovered the flesh it had lost and showed no sign of illness. Nor did physical weakness remain; the girl was able to climb stairs just as if she had never been ill. Later X-rays and blood tests confirmed that the tuberculosis had left her. A number of depositions were made by neighbours who had been at the house, attesting the sudden healing they had witnessed.

Some details of the incident have been obscured by the passage of years and by the astonishing nature of the main facts. Was it significant that her stepfather was the first person sought by the girl after her healing? Had her adolescent relations with him been stormy and perhaps a contributory factor in her illness? Was a reconciliation with him central to the process of being healed?

What the girl herself described to the fascinated, and growing, audience of neighbours and wellwishers, was hearing her name called by an angel, the 'Angel of the Lord'. He called her name three times and she replied "I am listening". He said "Dorothy, your sufferings are over. Get up and walk." Obeying these instructions — as it were supported by the vision — she got up and walked out of the room.

Inevitably the news spread. Reporters arrived, one of them, from the *Daily Chronicle*, who remembered, years later, how he had called to see the girl who was miraculously healed, and found her sitting in front of the fire wrapped in blankets (after several years in bed she had no clothes which fitted her). 'I remember telling my parents you looked exactly like some pictures of the Virgin Mary. There was the same type of feature and your face bore such a lovely expression of Divine beauty and peace. I remember it as well as if I had only seen you yesterday.'

The parallel that he makes is an interesting one, the parallel with the young, simple girl who received the announcement of the Angel Gabriel. Because of her lack of 'normal' experience of the world, no doubt, there is something simple and naïve that comes out in all the early descriptions of Dorothy Kerin. Accounts of her healing experience all stress her extreme youth so assiduously that it is a surprise to discover that it is not a seventeen-year-old who had the experience, but a young woman of twenty-three years old, an age at which many women were married and had several children of their own. But with this young woman one senses that adolescence was not yet complete, that the long years of cruel illness had slowed her maturity. On the other hand she had had an experience that most adolescents do not have — the experience of prolonged suffering and pain, culminating in a remarkable event full of a profoundly religious awareness. She may have been naïve in the ways of the world, but in the ways of the spirit she had travelled fast and far. It is this kind of one-sided development, usually forced by circumstances, that we note so often in the saints, and, one might add, in geniuses of all kinds.

Those who have unique spiritual experiences at once encounter a very great problem, what the Christians have called 'pride', and what Jung called 'inflation'. If the experience is unique then one is, in some sense, 'special', and if one is 'special' how does one live without a sense of self-congratulation, a heightened self-consciousness that is at once inimical to the self-forgetfulness which is the road of the spirit? Dorothy Kerin, like the young Bernadette, was exposed immediately and brutally to this dilemma, as sensation-seekers began to pursue her. According to contemporary accounts, sixty people came to the Kerin front door on the first day after the newspaper reports appeared, and a hundred on the second day, while crowds gathered just to see the house. Not perceiving the inherent callousness of those who love 'signs and wonders', the young woman patiently told her story over and over again. Four days later a London specialist, Dr. Edwin Ash, who had taken a particular interest in the case, invited her to come and stay at his home, partly so that further tests could be made, partly, no doubt, to give her respite from the intolerable publicity her healing had evoked, and she stayed in Portman Square for six weeks.

In June, 1912, four months after her miraculous healing, she wrote a 'message' which appeared in a paper called *The Weekly Budget*. It is a moving document, unworldly and slightly purple in its language (but the difficulty of talking about spiritual experience has defeated more practised writers than Dorothy Kerin) but deeply humble, in spite of the onslaught of public acclaim she had received. There is a very strong sense of her own vocation — a vocation as yet only partly revealed to her so far as its practical outworking was concerned — and she has no false humility about admitting this. Her sense of her threefold mission — to heal the sick, to comfort the sorrowing, and to bring faith to the faithless — to which she refers at the beginning was to remain with her throughout her life. Side by side with this, and the key to her humility, is her conviction that healing and joy is meant for all men, not for a special few, and that her own healing is a kind of sign, and that she is no more than an instrument. Just how difficult it must have been to maintain her human poise in the face of all that had happened is shown in the story she tells of the man who wanted to touch her in order to be healed. She had become, for some of her contemporaries, a Christ figure, as she was later to be for many others, and the temptation to 'inflation' must at times have been very great.

> The message began: In my restoration to health I have been entrusted with a message for the whole world, a promise of healing to the sick, comfort to the sorrowing and faith to the faithless. This message is for everybody as soon as they are ready to accept it and have the desire.
>
> How these things are going to be brought into practice has not been revealed to me yet. I only know that it will depend largely upon Prayer and Faith. I do know there is a beautiful truth for us as soon as we are ready for it.
>
> I am confident that as soon as people are brought to open their spiritual eyes, these great and beautiful manifestations will be for them also. The vast multitude build up a barrier between the seen and the unseen — between spiritual beauty and themselves — by worldly lives and by foolishness, but as soon as this barrier is broken down there will be a great inrush of spiritual beauty and glory. I have seen it and I know.

People do not realise that the spiritual part is much the greater portion. It is the true inheritance of all, but we do not claim it . . . I believe we are on the threshold of a great revelation from the Spirit that is Infinite. I feel that man is about to have a great awakening. What strengthens me in my belief? Prayer . . . Prayer is the desire of the soul for spiritual things. There is a form of Prayer without words, a voiceless prayer in the heart, that God and God only understands . . . People say to me "What are you going to do with your life?" If you ask me what God is going to do with my life, I answer, "I do not know." It will come from God. One life lifted from the shadow of death and brought into the sunshine of happiness should be enough to convince the world . . . I know that it was not for me alone, but that there is a divine purpose in my being singled out to manifest the healing power of the spirit. God knows the way. I do not know. I know that whereas I was prostrate, now I am well. I am an instrument in God's hands . . .

Christ is as much alive today as He was when upon earth, and is sending His message to those who will receive it. I feel no weight of care. Life is radiant when it is rightly lived . . . The Spirit of the Infinite lives in the truth, and the truth should make us not only free but joyous. Religion should be like the song of the birds. The glories of existence are all about us. The ineffable Power of Infinite Life is ours for the taking. There is nothing to hinder us except our own blindness . . . It is possible for every door to open into Paradise. It is possible for every life to come into communion with the Infinite.

People say to me "Come out into the world and live," but I say, "Come out from the world and live," and by that I do not mean come out and live your life away from your fellows. The old idea that people should go into the mountain or into the deserts and serve God by shunning society has been proved a fallacy. To be of help to your fellows; to share their joys and have them share yours; to smile with them; and if possible to banish their tears, are efforts worth while. What I mean by coming out from the world is to put aside the worldly things that pamper for a moment and perish — things that leave the soul empty and seared. It is not a denial, not a renunciation, but the embracing of things that are supernal, things that are spiritual and do not die. The world has repeated for centuries, but without realizing the full significance of the thought, that God is everywhere, and that the Kingdom of Heaven is within us. I believe that the world is ready today for a complete revelation of the literal and beautiful truth of these sayings that have largely come to be formal in their endless repetition.

The great truth is that Power unlimited, sublime and free is within reach of us all.

Sometimes people in London come up to me in the street and speak to me. The other day a man came to me in the street and said, "Excuse me, Miss, but may I touch you, perhaps the Spirit of the Master may pass through you into me."

You must break down the barrier before the inrush of glory can come in. The Spirit of God cannot come into the soul that is not receptive. Wealth could not buy my experience. It could not have effected my cure. It is the Spirit, the Spirit of Jesus, the Living God, that has given me this New Life.

To be miraculously healed of a grave illness, to feel herself in close touch with God, to have a sense of vocation, made enormous demands on Dorothy Kerin. To begin with it invited a response which she longed to make, yet only by trial and error could she discover exactly what that response should be. Inevitably she took the path of all who have such experiences — she turned to prayer, to spiritual reading, and, so far as her life allowed, to solitude. She also received a large volume of correspondence — a burden which was to remain for most of the rest of her life. She also wrote a book about her experiences, *The Living Touch*, which was marked with her usual careful balance; she knew that she had in some sense been specially chosen, but also that she was 'ordinary'.

Behind so much spiritual insight and so much hope, however,

it is possible to guess at a very real human loneliness. Most human beings were not singled out by miracle; most women in their twenties were occupied with a more commonplace experience of love. Throughout Dorothy Kerin's life there are hints of a longing for 'normal' life, a longing which to some degree she achieved within the community at Burrswood; in the beginning, however, there was a real fear of this clashing with her vocation. What mattered most to her was to 'obey', wherever that obedience might lead her. Yet at this stage no very clear path seemed marked out for her. Patience, as well as loneliness, seemed to be required of the eager disciple.

There were not many ways open to her to express the love and longing she felt, to share her vision with mankind. One way, however, was in public speaking, and she accepted invitations to speak, many of them from spiritualist and theosophist organisations. The impression is that her faith at this time, though basically Christian, had no strong denominational bias; this may have fostered a certain naïvety in her, but it also left her free of the contempt for other shades of belief which have so often marred Christians, and delightfully open to all who were earnestly seeking.

In 1915, when she was twenty-five, she met Dr. Langford-James at the house of a friend. An Anglo-Catholic priest much older than Dorothy Kerin, with a strong interest in mystical theology, he was deeply interested in her experiences and concerned for her future spiritual development. Also, with the peculiar intensity of the period which, all these years later, is so hard to identify with, he felt a need to place and keep this remarkable soul safe in the Catholic fold. He became her confessor and began to advise her about prayer and about her spiritual reading.

From their first encounter, Dorothy Kerin was obviously very drawn to Dr. Langford-James. Much later he was to describe their relationship as that of father and daughter, and this undoubtedly gives the clue to the strong influence he had upon her. The relationship with her father, so sharply and harshly broken off at the age of twelve, had found a continuation in the person of the fatherly adviser. The fascination was mutual,

Dr. Langford-James clearly enjoying the sort of Pygmalion-role that fell to his lot in shaping and moulding the spiritual development of this docile and rather childlike pupil.

Later in the same year Dr. Langford-James and his wife invited Dorothy Kerin to come and make her home with them in their Vicarage at Enfield, so that she could pursue her life of prayer and of quiet, under the priest's expert guidance and away from the more robust pressures of her own family household. She accepted and began a life in the much more pious atmosphere of the Langford-James' household, where there was a chapel of the Blessed Sacrament at the top of the house, and where all the niceties of Anglo-Catholic practice were observed. Langford-James saw himself in the classic mould of spiritual director, and expected 'obedience' from his pupil. Later in their acquaintance he suggested that she take 'simple vows' (of poverty, chastity and obedience), a wish to which she acceded.

But it was not, after all, within the framework of monastery or convent that Dorothy Kerin was living the 'religious' life, and there were none of the safeguards of community insight and community criticism. The young woman had a strong unconscious attraction to the priest because of her need for a father-figure, and no doubt, the 'daughter' exerted an equally strong unconscious attraction for him. One wonders how Mrs. Langford-James felt about this strong relationship *à deux*; it is possible to feel sympathy for her later outbreaks of bitterness which eventually drove Dorothy Kerin out of her house.

However, in the beginning the pleasure of being cared for and understood and so released from the loneliness of her very special experience must have been very great. She experienced great joy in prayer, and many of what are called 'graces'. The curious intensity of life in the Langford-James' household was accompanied by many phenomena which seem strange in the twentieth century, but were commonplaces of mystical experience among the Christian saints. Dorothy Kerin saw a crucifix shining with light, she found her bed strewn with flowers that were not to be found locally, her dog who had been run over was miraculously healed. She saw, and had conversations with, the Devil, she had visions of the Virgin Mary, and of the Holy Family at

Bethlehem, and during the First World War she had out-of-the-body experiences finding herself actually in France amid the mud and horror of the trenches while praying for soldiers at the Front.

The most remarkable of all these experiences was that, on the Feast of the Immaculate Conception in 1915, she received the Stigmata. The marks were preceded by the most intense pain, first in her left hand, after which a red spot gradually appeared there. On the next day she received the marks in her side and in her right hand, both preceded by great pain, and on the following day she received the wounds in her feet. Dr. Langford-James invited fellow-priests and others whom he trusted, to come and witness to these marks (apparently much to Dorothy Kerin's distress) and more than one spoke of seeing in the palm of the hand a projection as if something sharp was pushing through the flesh.

During the period that Dorothy Kerin spent in the Langford-James' household she passed through many stages of prayer, stages of ecstatic joy and vision, and stages of desolation and spiritual dereliction. Dorothy Arnold has compared this to the path described by St. John of the Cross — the illuminative way, followed by the unitive way, and culminating in Spiritual Marriage. There is no doubt that Dorothy Kerin was 'married' to the person of Christ — both given to and totally identified with — giving herself to the relationship with a thoroughness that few people married in the more mundane way give themselves to their partners.

Throughout these years she suffered dreadful physical health. She was the victim of heart trouble, of mysterious haemorrhages from her lungs (X-ray plates revealed no trace of tuberculosis), headaches, influenza and 'chills'. Yet at other times she seemed astonishingly robust, as when, on a trip to North Wales, she and her spiritual director attempted a full mountain climb together, a baffling piece of information since she had gone to Wales suffering from 'physical weakness'. Throughout her life she was singularly lacking in physical cautiousness, and this perhaps was why she was so accident-prone. (Amid the other sufferings of her life at this period she was bitten by a viper and severely affected by its venom and attacked by a robber in a lonely stretch of countryside, who attempted to steal her handbag.) In the case of her illnesses it seems likely that she tended to 'convert' mental suffering into physical suffering, and to experience as pain and weakness emotions which she could not, at that stage of her life, consciously experience.

Suddenly, in 1929, a remarkable change came over her life. She was forty years old, something of a landmark in most people's lives, as they begin to face what life has or has not offered them in terms of personal relationships or professional success. In Dorothy's case, life was not going to offer her marriage, or motherhood. (She was later to say that she had not wanted the first, but had very much wanted the second.) It was still not clear how she was to fulfil her very strong sense of vocation. She had spent years learning to pray, practising intercession, helping with the many 'good works' around the parish, but this did not seem to be the outworking of the three-fold mission to which she had once believed herself called.

It is probable too that she had outgrown her 'father-figure'. The years of living with the Langford-James's had filled that wounding gap in her childhood, and now, so much later than most people, she was at last ready to 'leave home', to stand on her own feet. The initial step of leaving the Langford-James's was not very dramatic — she moved out of their home and went to live with her mother and brother at Ealing — but it was the beginning of Dorothy Kerin's life as an independent person, and very soon it was to take on a shape that was entirely characteristic of her.

2

AT CULMINGTON ROAD in Ealing Dorothy Kerin rented a ten room house which she called St. Raphael and opened it as a Home of Healing. No doubt in the long years she had spent with the Langford-James's some such idea had been forming in her mind and now the moment had come to start her life's work. Many friends rallied round with gifts of furniture and money and soon she was ready to open her doors. Her first patient was Gwen Williams (Dorothy was later to refer to her as 'my first child') now on the staff of Burrswood.

> I had trained to be a missionary, and then wasn't strong enough to go abroad and I was very upset about it. It really made me ill and there were other things that had happened that were very emotionally upsetting. A priest friend said to me that he knew a very nice person and that it would be very good for me to go and spend ten days with her. So I went not knowing anything about her. And though I'd been going to be a missionary, and convert the world, I didn't believe a word she said about her healing to begin with! I thought "Good heavens, I think I must have come to the house of a mad woman", though her mother and brother had been there at the meal beforehand, and they were quite normal and the meal had been quite normal. But then she took me into the little sitting-room and began telling me this. It came as quite a shock. I said to her "Please don't tell me any more because I don't believe it." When I went up to bed I didn't know what to do. I thought, well I'll have to make some excuse tomorrow morning to go. And then at breakfast everything was so normal, — Dorothy teased me and called me 'Pooh' because I said I loved honey — and I thought to myself perhaps it won't do any harm to stay on. Perhaps she's only mad on that one point! And so I continued. But by the end of the week I was longing for her to tell me the story of her

healing, but she never did. And something stopped me from asking her. I felt I couldn't.

Later on that holiday Dorothy Kerin asked Gwen Williams to go for a walk with her and the setter Bruno across Walpole Park, because she wanted to show her something. 'We stopped and she pointed to a large house, and said "That's what I wanted to show you." I said "What a nice house" and she said "I'm going to have that house." I said "But Dorothy, you can't, you haven't got enough money." She said "Oh, I know I'm going to have it because Our Lord's told me." '

Distrustful as she had felt at her first encounter with Dorothy Kerin, Gwen Williams had very quickly come to like and trust her, impressed as many others were to be later by the humour, the gaiety, and the underlying confidence in what she was drawn to do. The inauspicious meeting developed into a life-long friendship.

Dorothy Kerin did buy the house in Mattock Lane that she had pointed out to Gwen Williams. The owner had wanted £5,000 for it, but reduced the price to £3,700 when he discovered the use it was to be put to. Many who believed in Dorothy and her work were eventually to donate money to make this venture possible — a few hundred pounds here and there — but in an act either of impressive faith, or alarming folly (according to one's point of view) she had already committed herself to buying it. Chapel House, as she called it, opened in October 1930. She owed £500 to the bank, to be repaid in December, from sources as yet uncertain, and she needed a lot of money for repairs and furnishings. Yet already she was talking of buying five other houses in the immediate locality to extend the work of Chapel House. The pent-up vitality of the years of preparation was ready to pour out in the work she had chosen.

Chapel House rapidly filled up with sick and Dorothy Kerin proceeded to engage trained nurses. On the advice of a doctor who sent patients to her she decided to register the house as a nursing home and so charge fees. This sensible step, somehow typical of the shrewdness which, as time went on was the inseparable companion of her 'otherworldliness', gave her a regular income which she could use both to extend the work and to take in patients who could not afford fees.

Another characteristic on which many would remark, became marked about this time. She was insistent that her houses must be places beautiful to look at, in which furnishings, drapery, etc. pleased the eye. Partly perhaps it was an instinct for the therapy given by beautiful surroundings, as an antidote to the boredom of days spent in bed, and the impersonality of many hospitals and institutions. But to Gwen Williams, on one of the walks they took in Walpole Park, Dorothy Kerin expressed her feelings on the subject in terms of her relationship with 'Our Lord'.

'She said to me "I want to make it as beautiful as possible, because it's for Our Lord. People so often give him their left-overs — the things they don't really want. I want to give him the very best that I possibly can." '

One of the nurses she took on at about this time was Rose Friend, a nursing sister who had trained at St. Bartholomew's, who heard about Dorothy Kerin's venture at a tea-party, was fired with enthusiasm, and rang her up the next morning. They took to one another at a first meeting, and Rose Friend agreed to come and work for her as soon as she was free from outstanding commitments. At this period, and throughout her life, Dorothy Kerin managed to attract the help of doctors and nurses of the finest quality, who saw in what she was attempting to do not any negation of their own skills and methods, but rather an added dimension which made their work doubly effective. As a doctor who discovered Dorothy Kerin's work at Burrswood was to say 'It was medicine under ideal conditions.'

An early, and staunch, friend of Dorothy Kerin's at Ealing was Dr. Helena King, the local G.P.

> I was asked by the Vicar of St. Barnabas if I would take another patient. I said yes, and he said "You will find her not quite like the ordinary patient!" And how right he was. I got to know her very well. At first I had to see her quite a bit because she had a high temperature and a 'flu germ and she wasn't taking care of herself at all, so I made her go to

bed and I looked after her for a bit as her G.P. Then I gradually got to know her better, and I thought she was a wonderful person. I was completely in sympathy with her work, in fact, I was thrilled to find that it went together with medicine. I thought that medicine and the way she practised her healing were a wonderful combination.

Chapel House became, almost at once, an instant success. It was full of patients, and many others, who had heard of Dorothy Kerin, came there to pour out their troubles and to seek out her advice. It was the beginning of the remarkable work of listening and counselling that was to continue until her death more than thirty years later. Those who could not come in person wrote to her, and answering letters made ever heavier calls on her time. Between getting Chapel House on its feet, furnished to her own exacting standards, and properly organised for the care of the sick; between that set of duties and the ever-greater demands that were being made upon her by letter and visit, she became ever more busy. The long hours of quiet and prayer she had enjoyed in the past were no longer available to her, except late at night or very early in the morning. Inevitably she got too little sleep.

The strains of setting up Chapel House and the period of over-working that followed led to an illness in which she was carefully and devotedly looked after by Rose Friend. It produced a close friendship between them which lasted for the rest of Rose Friend's life. She remained always very close to Dorothy Kerin, nursing her in illness, protecting her from the unending calls made by others upon her strength and her goodwill. It is not unusual for a genius in any field to need to be looked after; the kind of selflessness and unselfconsciousness needed for any great achievement means that the basic necessities of life — food, clothes, sleep, leisure — get overlooked. If such a person is lucky enough to find a friend who loves to tend them in that way — to take on, as it were, a motherly role on their behalf, then they are liberated to do what they feel they must. Dorothy Kerin's surviving friends speak of the late Rose Friend — Jummie, as she was generally known — with a sort of rueful gratitude, remembering her as a fierce watchdog who nevertheless made Dorothy Kerin's life better and easier by her care.

Under her care, Dorothy Kerin recovered from illness and from then until the end of her life seemed to enjoy vastly improved health, which suggests an element of neurosis in the interminable sickness she suffered in the Langford-James household. Dr. King remembers not so much Dorothy Kerin's frailty, as the quite remarkable powers of recovery she possessed.

> She suffered from overstrain quite a lot. She would go on visiting and pouring herself out far beyond what most people can stand up to, and occasionally she would not be able to do any more at all and she'd have to knock off and go to bed for two or three days. She had the most remarkable powers of instantaneous recovery. She would be terribly bad, perhaps with a high temperature, completely drained out. I would say "You'll have to be in bed until this is over," and within a couple of days she would greet me with a beaming smile and say "I'm perfectly all right now. Thank you very much, I'm fine!" And nothing could stop her then.

Another faithful member of the present staff who joined Dorothy Kerin around this time was 'Bocky' Caudwell, who came as a young woman in her twenties, to work at the Ealing house as cook. Unlike others who stayed she did not begin with any particular moment of insight about Dorothy Kerin, nor did it occur to her that there was anything unusual about the place in which she was working. 'I might have left at any time while I worked at Ealing.' Only gradually did she begin to feel that her employer was a very remarkable woman and that her work was no ordinary work. She cannot remember when or how this knowledge came to her, but gradually she was drawn into a deepening loyalty until she became one of the handful of women who worked alongside Dorothy Kerin for the rest of her life.

The Home of Healing was such a success that it was possible to buy a second house, St. Michael's, and gradually to buy five other houses in Mattock Lane. When she needed a chaplain for the Home, Dorothy Kerin's former director, Dr. Langford-

James, was eager to take on the job, but having made herself independent of his guidance, she could not re-open that chapter of her life. Another father, some say a brother-figure, Philip Loyd, Bishop of Nasik in India, later to be Bishop of St. Albans, had become important to her, and the letters of his which survive show a moving gentleness for her and an understanding of the burden she carried. There is no taste of 'direction' in them but rather of the encouragement, interest and concern one may show for an 'equal' who is also a close friend. They compared notes about the very difficult work each had to do, certain of the other's understanding.

What, we may wonder, made this nursing home so very different from others where the sick are nursed back to health after operation or illness? Certainly the laying-on of hands was practised, and the work was surrounded and upheld by prayer and Christian belief, though at Ealing, as later at Burrswood, this was never in any way thrust upon patients; it was simply there for them to draw upon or lean upon if they wished to do so. Not all the staff could as yet have had the dedication or the vision of treating the 'whole' person that was later to be so striking at Burrswood, but at the centre of the growing project was a woman who knew that sickness is often allied to emotional problems, who was prepared to listen, quietly and selflessly, and who had strange, vivid insights into what was ailing people. Perhaps the key to the healing effect she had, to which so many have later testified, was that she saw the individual's suffering in the perspective of trust in the will of God; 'healing' was not the first consideration, but obedience.

> Gwen Williams remembers: She never talked about healing to me. I sometimes was quite ill when I came, but what I understood her to believe — it wasn't so much what she said — was that if Our Lord was going to heal one then he would. Also she never once said "Oh so and so had the same illness as you and they got better" — she treated you as an individual.

'She was so completely possessed with "living with God" as

you might say' Dr. King remembers. 'It was absolutely natural with her.'

Dr. King saw the effect Dorothy Kerin had on some of her seriously ill patients at Ealing. She remembers only a few cases where the results were so extraordinary as to approach what most people think of as a miracle, but feels that the method Dorothy Kerin used for treating sickness was exactly right.

> I think all doctors ought to work in association with someone who believes in the healing grace of God . . . One does realise that quite a lot of one's patients have stresses underlying their illnesses. The more you know of them, and their family life, and their background, you know that there is an underlying anxiety.

Prayer and the 'laying-on of hands' seemed to combine naturally with medical treatment (itself, perhaps, a different sort of 'laying-on of hands').

'I think it is what Dorothy used to say — that a channel is opened by which the healing grace of God can come to the person who is prayed for or who has the laying-on of hands. It seems to me quite reasonable that there should be healing there.'

Dr. King's words recall the words of Leslie Weatherhead on the subject of miracle in *Psychology, Religion and Healing*. 'A miracle is a law-abiding event whereby God accomplishes his redemptive purposes through the release of energies which belong to a plane of being higher than any with which we are normally familiar.'

The basic pattern of Dorothy Kerin's life-work — caring for the sick, counselling the distressed, witnessing to her own very vivid religious faith — the triple commission she had foreseen in her girlhood, was now established in the very remarkable centre at Ealing. Yet, whether she knew it or not, she was moving towards a fuller expression of her vision of healing, and was gathering round her the faithful nucleus of workers who would come to Burrswood. In 1936 Marina Chavchavadze, daughter of a distinguished Russian family exiled by the Revolution, had come to stay at Chapel House as the result of an illness, and in the course of the next year or two discovered a vocation to work with Dorothy Kerin.

Dorothy Kerin's friends from this period of her life constantly recall her humour, her infectious laugh, her capacity to surprise them by saying the unexpected thing, and her unassuming gentleness. Her smallness and frailty also often impressed itself on them. But there was something irrepressible about her — 'she *enjoyed* life so' said one — as if everything was fun, 'a lark', and she loved setting off on a 'trip' or holiday, usually accompanied by one of her unending succession of dogs.

The outbreak of war did not at first greatly affect life at Chapel House. Another, private, event, initially disrupted Dorothy Kerin's life far more. In 1941 she adopted a baby, Anne. This was not perhaps in itself a great surprise to her friends who knew of her love and longing for babies. The surprise was to come. Gwen Williams remembers visiting Dorothy Kerin at Chapel House and watching her give Anne her bath.

> I said to her, "You won't only adopt one child, will you? It will be so lonely."
>
> And she said "Oh no, I'm going to adopt nine. Our Lord's told me so."
>
> I said, "Dorothy, you can't possibly do that."
>
> She said "I'm going to." And she did, you see.

In the course of a year she adopted eight other boys and girls, two pairs of twins amongst them. So many years later it is not easy to know what to make of this action. Since those days there has been a lot of research on child development, and children may now no longer be adopted by a single person since ideally a child needs both a father and a mother. In the forties it was generally believed that anything that took a child out of an institutional atmosphere and from the stigma of being 'an orphan' was automatically a good thing. Nowadays we tend to see the importance of putting children into 'normal' home conditions, and by the standards of normal living i.e. a house with Dad and Mum, Mum regarding the children as her chief work in life; the Kerin household fell very far short, despite the enormous amount of love and care Dorothy Kerin expended on the children. She had foreseen the difficulty of the absent father.

'She told me she was going to bring them up with God as their father' Gwen Williams remembers. 'Now that sounds marvellous, and I thought it was wonderful at the time, but now I incline to think that children want a father that's a bit more concrete. Of course I realised that she was doing what she did in the belief that it was God's will — so that she could do no other.'

Even if one can understand the overriding longing for a child or children, the mind boggles at the decision to adopt nine babies, all more or less the same age. Few ordinary mothers would contemplate such an undertaking — indeed, nature mercifully makes it impossible — but for Dorothy Kerin to attempt it, at the age of fifty two, when already deeply and totally committed to an exacting job which left her very little free time, must seem to some an act of folly, or an unconscious compensation for not having borne a child.

What it meant in practice was that none of the children enjoyed that sense of being their mother's undisputed darling which is every baby's birthright. They had to share her love with eight siblings at the same stage of development and it is not surprising that they grew up wild and aggressive beyond the normal wildness of small children.

'They were absolute little savages', Kathleen Burke-Collis remembers of her first encounter with them when they were about five, and others who had already tried to care for them had given a similar verdict.

In the early stages of their development Dorothy Kerin's friends helped her financially so that she could employ nannies to undertake the heavy physical task of caring for nine children. Later, friends such as Bocky, Kathleen, Marina and Peggy Simpson, all played a valiant part in bringing them up, and eventually the children went off to boarding school. To do Dorothy Kerin justice, she had never intended that the children should go to school until they had reached Public School age but the complete collapse of Governess-control precipitated decisions which had to be made with painful speed. There is no doubt that Dorothy Kerin loved each one of them dearly, was prepared to work her fingers to the bone for them, and devote every second of her scanty free time to their happiness and well-being. Yet one must doubt whether it was in her power to offer the conditions, simple as they are, that little children need for happy and successful growth. Also, whether for all her wealth of loving and maternal feeling, she could really enter into the way little children think and feel. There is an alarming story, reported by Kathleen Burke-Collis, published in Dorothy Arnold's biography, of Dorothy Kerin suddenly informing all the children at once that they were adopted on, of all occasions, the day before they were due to start school.

> On the eve of their starting their first term at Forest Row, Mummy said she wanted to speak to them. So, when they had all had their baths, they collected in the room at the top of the backstairs . . . She started off by telling them that she herself had never been to school, but that she thought they would love it. They would hear lots of things they had never heard before. There would be beautiful things, and things that were not beautiful, but they must try hard to remember only the beautiful. They probably would hear they were adopted children. "Now" she said, "I want to tell you that it is a very special thing to be adopted, because it means that you were wanted very much, and that Jesus himself is your Father. He chose you and sent you to me to look after. Therefore, if anyone says anything to you about being adopted, always remember that you are very specially Jesus' children . . ."
>
> "But . . . Mummy, aren't you our *real* Mummy?"
>
> And then the howls began. John started off, but very soon they were all, without exception, howling.

Both the distance of Dorothy Kerin as a mother (one of the children, as an adolescent, was to complain to one of the staff that he had to make an appointment to see his mother), and perhaps a streak of sentimentality that made it hard for her to see children as people (hence the suggestion that they should remember only the beautiful) led to the unconsciously cruel action of suddenly springing the knowledge of adoption on children already under the stress of starting school.

Not surprisingly, the children did suffer a stormy development, and it was perhaps all the stormier because of the conviction of some of Dorothy Kerin's friends, that in the circumstances they should have turned out 'perfect children'. They had less than most children, however, in terms of individual love and attention, and their lives could not be easy.

What then, are we to make of Dorothy Kerin's conviction that their adoption was 'Our Lord's will'? Some people suggest that her conviction of God's will, though often impressively borne out by events, was not infallible, and if there is one area where a woman may be influenced much more than she knows by unconscious wishes, it is in the wish to have children. The decision to adopt 'the nine' as they have often been called, brought Dorothy Kerin enormous joy and fulfilment, and also enormous strain, hurt, and towards the end, I would guess, bewilderment, that her relationship with them was no longer close and rich. She had, in fact, 'given' herself to a vocation quite as exacting as childbearing and rearing, and perhaps underestimated the extent to which motherhood would make equally absolute demands.

As time went on, life at Ealing became too confining for the children, and through the gift of a friend, Gladys Modin, a comfortable country house at Speldhurst in Kent became available to Dorothy Kerin. Life in the country suited the children, and Dorothy Kerin found that she, too, enjoyed it tremendously. She had always loved dogs, and now the enthusiasm spread to horses. With considerable courage she learned to ride so that she could join the children on horseback. Peggy Simpson, who looked after the horses, remembers this as rather a harrowing experience for those who had to look on.

> Personally, I found it terrifying going out with her, because she was mostly much too tired to cope with it, and though she loved it it was late in life to take it up. She hadn't really

got the physical strength to hold on with her knees and that kind of thing. I couldn't stop her falling off, and she did! And she invariably hurt herself. She used to fall heavily. I found it an ordeal and I longed for it to be over! But she so adored the horses, and she had terrific pluck.

Remembering Dorothy Kerin's invalid adolescence it is moving to think of her embarking on the sort of youthful pursuit she had been denied.

At Speldhurst too there was opportunity for walking, gardening, and the pleasures of country life, and there was more time to enjoy the children than there had been at Ealing. However, half the week was spent at the nursing home at Ealing, until the strain of this dual life became too much, and she decided, encouraged by friends, that the answer might be to buy a larger country house, with room for both children and patients. The Kerin family already knew Groombridge as a result of attending the local church and Dorothy Kerin learned that a big house there called Burrswood was empty. In 1948 she moved to Burrswood with a faithful handful of workers — Bocky, Marina, Kathleen, Peggy and Ruth — and moved the sick and aged patients from Ealing to the house at Speldhurst. The most important phase of her work had now begun.

3

BURRSWOOD HAD, IN its day, been a rather splendid property, owned by, amongst other wealthy people, the Grand Duke Michael of Russia. Part of the house was said to have been designed by Decimus Burton, and it had a most beautiful aspect, facing south over the Kentish Weald. It had stood in 250 acres of land, and had had fine gardens which, in its hey-day, had needed the labour of fifteen gardeners.

By the end of the war, however, it was in a deplorable state. Much of the land had been sold off. The gardens were overgrown, and the house had been occupied by the Army, and then severely damaged by a V1 that dropped in the grounds. It had had two post-war owners in quick succession, one of whom had begun repair work and then given up from lack of money. The poor state of the property meant that it was for sale for £8,000, an amount possible to raise by the sale of the Ealing property, but there was a backbreaking amount of work to be done before the house would be habitable and the gardens restored to even a fraction of their former glory.

Initially with the aid of German prisoners and a gardener from Ealing, but eventually, largely by the efforts of her small group of devoted workers — Kathleen, Marina, Bocky, Ruth — the house and garden were brought into a tolerable condition. Bocky remembers what very hard work it was.

> We never went to bed before midnight, but however hard we worked, Dorothy always worked harder. She was up hours before the rest of us. She never let us sag. Sometimes, after an enormous effort to get a piece of work finished, we would think "Now we can stop". Then Dorothy would say "Today we will do so-and-so" and we would all have to set to work again. I don't know how she found the strength, because she was really very frail, and the physical work must have been hard for her. Yet she kept us all going, and often made things seem fun when they were very hard work. She would say

"Let's all go and make bonfires." It wasn't fun, but she made it so.

The unceasing work made tempers very frayed among Dorothy's staff, and more than one of them remembers the rows that used to blow up between them. 'Many's the fish-cake I've thrown at X!' Yet they also remember their pioneering work with joy and pride. 'It was wonderful being able to take part in the building up of this place. As I grow older I realise more and more what a lot we gained from just being with Dorothy.'

Perhaps some of the joy came from that special sense of daring and high spirits that women often have when they run a project, as if there is something miraculous and wonderfully stimulating about achieving something without male help. There is an almost schoolgirlish high spirit about some of the exploits of the Kerin household; however hard the work, or tragic the prevalence of sickness and grief, there was an irrepressible sense of fun about the place which nearly everyone who lived there mentions.

Then again there was the growing sense of community between all of them. In the forties people did not think very much in terms of communities, except of the traditional religious type, and there is no evidence that Dorothy Kerin saw herself as setting out to build a community. Yet the trial and error of the Ealing and Speldhurst period had led her to this development, one which was to be of great significance for the future of Burrswood. In those days people did not know very much of the theories of community living — of the devastating loves and hates which can arise when people are together all the time — but their strong sense of belief in Dorothy Kerin's work, and their love and devotion to her as a person, made it possible for all these women to continue together. As with all one-sex communities it is tempting to wonder when we speak of love, are we talking about her followers having a 'crush' on Dorothy Kerin? In some cases it is clear that this was, for a time at least, part of the friendship, not altogether surprisingly since for a number of those closest to Dorothy Kerin, her intervention in their lives had saved them from chronic sickness or intractable emotional problems, and brought them to a much more fulfilling way of life.

Judging by the evidence of her life her closest relationships were always with women and not with men. Men were father-figures — as with Dr. Langford-James, Bishop Loyd and other clerical advisers — or they played a brotherly role as co-workers, as doctors and others who helped her were later to do. Those with whom she spent her leisure hours, went on holiday, lived and set up a community with, and confided in most deeply, were women. Some of them did feel a very deep tie with her, in particular it seems the tie of the disciple for the master (or mistress), which made it a pleasure for them to put in hours of selfless work. Others, and this included a very wide circle outside, as well as inside, the community, saw her as a friend, but a very remarkable friend, engaged upon work with which they could not fail to be impressed. It was her special gift to weld these different sorts of love into a unity which served as a basis for the work of healing. Perhaps the measure of her success was the extent to which her workers overcame feelings of jealousy and rivalry, and learned a deep sympathy and tolerance for those whose temperament or social background was utterly different from their own.

One of the difficulties in assessing the development of Burrswood is the impression one gets that, during the forties and fifties, Dorothy Kerin was very much 'taken up' by society, supported in her work by titled and wealthy ladies, perhaps even pursued by the kind of rich, but idle, patron who likes to dabble in religion, particularly when, as in the case of religion allied to healing, it smacks of the esoteric. Dorothy Kerin has been much criticised on these grounds, and for using the money given to her by such friends to buy beautiful antiques and furnishings to decorate her houses and the church. Perhaps more seriously, she allowed friends drawn to her by her work to dress her children in the height of Kensington Gardens fashion, and eventually to pay for their education at well-known public schools. To all this Dorothy Kerin would probably have given the same answer that she had before to Gwen Williams, some years previously. 'People so often give Him their left-overs —

the things that they don't really want. I want to give Him the best I possibly can' — This was the root of all her giving and planning.

It seems to me that we must note first of all the profound change that has taken place in our society since the forties. The active support of 'society' was essential to a charitable enterprise at that time in a way that would be unnecessary today (though most charities feel the need still for influential patrons, choosing them now from the ranks of the meritocracy, rather than the aristocracy), and Dorothy Kerin needed her titled ladies as she needed the help and support of bishops and clerics. As word spread among them many of them did come to Dorothy Kerin with their sicknesses and their spiritual problems, and were genuinely helped by her. (As a friend of Dorothy's whom I interviewed remarked 'The rich have problems just as much as the poor!'.) It seemed natural and right that they should show their gratitude by making gifts or legacies to her.

But I think we should note in Dorothy Kerin a mixture of shrewdness and naïvety (perhaps what Christ meant when he said his disciples should be wise as serpents and harmless as doves) that encouraged this development. If she was to help as many people as she wanted to do then she did need money, much more money than she could charge in nursing home fees. She wanted to help those who could not afford to pay — that was part of her vision — and she wanted to fill the lives of the sick and the sad with a glimpse of beauty. If it was the sort of beauty which, at that time, was associated with well-to-do country houses, that didn't really matter. In a sense wealth and beauty were everyone's property, a glimpse of the kingdom. So, she accepted the devotion of rich and influential friends, bought and sold houses in a sensible business-like way, and combed antique shops to buy objects as rare as the alabaster box, with money which might have been given to the poor, particularly in the hungry thirties.

Yet there was also something naïve and childlike about Dorothy Kerin which took it as in a sense her due if people showered her with cheques, beautiful objects, and the wherewithal to clothe and educate nine children. As I read accounts of these floods of giving, written either by her or by her friends I find it difficult not to feel exasperated by the ingenuous way in which her expectation of help is couched in terms of divine intervention. On one or two occasions cheques for needed amounts of money were written out and left on the altar for God to honour them, and within a day or two He usually did so in the person of a wealthy friend receiving a legacy at just the right moment.

Yet this leaning upon the generosity of others, and slight fecklessness about where money was to come from (both, in my view, necessary for the start of any considerable enterprise) were the reflection of something utterly generous and daring in Dorothy Kerin's own character. Content herself to live on very little — although she loved clothes, she wore the same ones year after year — she gave recklessly of her own possessions, energy and time. As is often the case with such people, she thought that others were similarly built. She perhaps did not know that the ceaseless giving which was the strength (and weakness) of her own character created difficulties for others.

One difficulty was that it turned her, at least for a time, into something of a cult figure, a cult of which there are disturbing traces to this day. People give generously to those who have charisma (something Dorothy Kerin undoubtedly had) and the more they give the more they fall under the spell of the cult. The central figure of the cult becomes the vehicle for 'projection'; the members of the cult find in him or her an unrecognised part of themselves, and not realising that this is so, devote themselves to the cult-figure with an uncritical and slavish devotion. Dorothy Kerin gave many a sense of the numinous, of the possibility of a relationship with God, hitherto quite unrealised in their lives, and it is not surprising that so many turned to her, often quite uncritically.

Yet, as always with Dorothy Kerin, one feels that she is saved by her humour, by a down-to-earth quality that knows better than to accept herself at others' valuation. She received the gifts, she gave her rich friends value for their money in terms of caring and listening to them, yet she managed to go free of pressures and cults. She was genuinely unsnobbish — rich and poor had equal claims upon her sympathy and help. Burrswood was, and is, remarkable, in transcending social boundaries, perhaps a more remarkable achievement in the forties than it is today. Dr. Elliott, her G.P. from when she first came to Burrswood, and a good friend and adviser, felt that at one stage there was a danger of her being taken up by the wrong people, a danger that was later averted.

> She tended to collect around her — because of her magnetism and her extraordinary powers — the wealthy, the people who had got too much time on their hands and wanted something unusual, the rather emotional types and sometimes even hysterical types. For a time the work was not on a matter-of-fact plane. That's what outside people used to think, and I had some difficulty in correcting this idea.

Dr. Elliott, a family doctor in Crowborough with a branch surgery in Groombridge, visited Burrswood in 1948 to advise upon a drug addict Dorothy Kerin was caring for.

> After I had seen the patient we chatted for a while about her, and then suddenly out of the blue Miss Kerin said "Would you be doctor to me and my family?" I didn't know anything about her at the time, but I soon realised that here was a completely remarkable woman. She was so remarkable that she got one to talk and enthuse about one's ideas almost straight away. I felt that this was the type of place, and hers was the sort of work, that G.P.s were looking for, namely practising medicine in the best possible circumstances. This was before Burrswood had become a nursing home.
>
> I had a tough time looking after the nine children — when one got measles the lot got measles — and I was the only man around at all, and I felt a strong sense of involvement with the place.
>
> There was intense opposition to Burrswood, not only in Groombridge, but from all the G.P.s and specialists around, because they regarded it at first as a crank place. There was almost open hostility from the specialists — they wouldn't

come here. I felt that my biggest contribution was simply to practise commonsense medicine here, so that I could show them that it wasn't a crackpot place. I found myself in a difficult position over it. It wasn't recognised as a nursing-home at first. Nobody who came here could get any help from their insurances — BUPA or PPP or anything like that ... Gradually, however, by talking to consultants, and managing to persuade them that it was a normal nursing home and that we did normal medicine here, and telling them about the work Miss Kerin did, it was possible to get them to start coming here. Then they started sending cases here, and we got it going as a nursing-home, and persuaded BUPA to accept it. There were times when she was having difficulty with staff that Miss Kerin wanted to give up having the nursing-home — she could never understand people who were not as totally dedicated as she was — but I used to say "For heaven's sake, don't do that. If anything happened to you, and there wasn't a nursing-home here and a fully trained staff, everything would collapse."

The task of restoring the beautiful house and furnishing it had been undertaken with great enthusiasm. Ruth Farr, who had joined Dorothy Kerin early in the forties after a long illness, found her feeling for beauty a kind of education.

'I came from a Quaker background and I had never come across anyone who felt beauty was important as she did.' In those days it seemed to go with a particular sort of High Anglican approach to life — the legacy from the Langford-James era. Certainly, Dorothy Kerin's expression of her faith was 'Catholic' — sacramental worship was at the heart of her belief, saints, and particularly the Virgin Mary, were important to her, she cared about traditional forms of worship, she was at home with imagery, with holy pictures, with crucifixes.

To those who never knew Dorothy Kerin and who may have grown up in a different religious tradition or no religious tradition at all, this can be slightly daunting, but it is interesting that her theological position never seemed any bar or obstacle to those who knew her.

Coming to a healing service presided over by Dorothy Kerin after many years of living in the East and a long experience of theosophy, Dorothy Arnold felt at once a sense of having 'come home', of having found what she was looking for. She feels that, as Dorothy Kerin grew older, her understanding and love for the adherents not only of other denominations but also of other religions grew, that she was able to perceive 'Christ' in them and respond with pleasure.

Certainly those who came to her for counsel never seemed conscious of denominational hurdles. What they describe is a woman who believed in the presence of Christ more, perhaps, than she believed in more ordinary reality and who looked at their problems in the light of that conviction. Many report the experience of finding that by the time they had recounted their troubles, the troubles had assumed a very different appearance. Others found they had no need to recount anything; just meeting Dorothy Kerin seemed to change the situation, or they felt that she knew the core of their suffering without further explanations. Some found themselves pouring out confessions of years of misspent life. Others were helped by a blunt comment which went straight to the heart of their problem.

"It's George that's wrong with you!" Dorothy Kerin remarked to a woman reduced by her husband's personality to a physical wreck. Through Burrswood this patient eventually found the will and the strength to struggle back to health and life, and even to continue with an impossible marriage.

In addition to the flood of people who came for counselling, there were the many who arrived incurably sick and dying.

And then there were the letters — perhaps the most exhausting and the least rewarding of all forms of human exchange, an endless burden which could not be evaded. Dorothy Arnold acted as Dorothy Kerin's secretary after 1956 thus helping with the burden, but it still took up an enormous amount of time. Bocky remembers that when Dorothy Kerin returned from shopping she would immediately sit down to her letters, and there, hours later, they would find her, still wearing the hat and coat she had not bothered to remove.

What exactly was the help she gave to all these needy people?

A clear, unshakable faith, a sense that everything was somehow 'all right', despite surface appearances, a first-hand experience of what it is like to be gravely, even terminally, ill. There was a buoyancy in her personality which conveyed itself even to those in extremes of despair. Dorothy Arnold remembers having the job of showing people in to Dorothy Kerin to seek her help and advice.

> Again and again I've seen people come into the hall looking distraught, haggard, at the end of their tether, hopeless many of them. I would show them into Dorothy's study. In ten minutes I have seen those same faces radiant, filled with a light which one can truly say was not a light of this world. What had happened? In ten minutes you cannot say very much to people who perhaps are suffering under a life-long disability or problem. My only explanation is that she brought Christ to them, that it was Christ's healing love and power that restored them to wholeness. I wouldn't say that all of them kept that wholeness, but for many, many of them, it was a turning-point.

Her staff rarely saw her broken by the suffering she witnessed so constantly. Sister Maria remembers her on one occasion coming out of the bedroom of a young mother with terminal cancer and saying "Why, why?" but she remembers it because of the surprise it caused her, though in a sense she found herself helped by this unexpected mood of rebellion against God's will. She was also capable of real toughness where she felt clinging and possessiveness was the problem with which she had to deal.

'She could be quite stern. She wasn't really the soft, gentle type. Under the velvet glove was a stiff iron hand, which she used when necessary.'

In addition to listening, counselling, answering letters and supervising the nursing-home in which every patient was treated with loving care, there were other kinds of help available to patients. One was the healing services which were regularly held, and during which anyone who wanted it could receive the laying-on of hands. Dorothy Kerin 'designed' this service herself in a form which continues to be practised to this day at Burrswood. The first words of the service are 'God is our hope and strength; a very present help in trouble', and hope and trust are the keynotes of the whole service. The service begins with thanksgiving for those who have been healed, and continues in prayer for the sick, for the work of Burrswood, for those who have requested prayers (a list of these lies upon the altar), and for those present at the service. There is silence, and then there is the Collect which has become the special prayer of the Burrswood Fellowship, with its deep longing for wholeness and healing.

O God, who hast prepared for them that love Thee
Such good things as pass man's understanding,
Pour into our hearts such love towards Thee
That we, loving Thee above all things,
May obtain thy Promises, which exceed all that we can desire,
Through Jesus Christ our Lord.

There is a lesson and music, and a singing of the 91st psalm.

Whoso dwelleth under the defence of the most High, shall abide under the shadow of the Almighty.
I will say unto the Lord, Thou art my hope, and my stronghold: my God, in Thee will I trust.

Then general confession and absolution, the Our Father, a prayer for those present to be healed, and a singing of the ancient hymn 'Come, Holy Ghost, our souls inspire'. (*Veni, creator spiritus*).

The priest goes to anyone who is unable to approach the altar and lays his hand upon their head with the words 'In the Name of God most High, and through His infinite love and power, may release from all sickness be given thee. In the Name of Jesus Christ our Saviour may the healing power of the Holy Spirit make you whole and keep you entire to the glory of God the Father.' Those who can go to the altar rail kneel and have the same words said to them.

Gwen Williams remembers coming to Burrswood after an accident in which she had fallen from a bus, and been found unconscious on the pavement. Shock and delayed concussion gave her nightmares and depression and a stutter, and in despair she went to Burrswood. The journey involved crossing London in a taxi and she discovered that she had acquired a terror of buses, and felt that they were 'coming at her'. 'I jumped from one end of the taxi to the other, like a pea in a pod.'

> When I got to Burrswood I was put to bed — Dorothy helped me undress — I was stuttering from the effort of the journey. For four or five days I stayed in bed, and then I got up and went to a healing service. I remember I burst into tears and two or three days after that I realised — quite simply — that I'd stopped having nightmares. In a fortnight's time I went home — all by myself — and I went across London in a taxi and never turned a hair at any of the buses!

Many go 'by proxy' to a healing service, at the request of friends who are too ill to come. Dr. Elliott often goes for patients and finds that for some, though not for all, it produces a beneficial change.

> There was one case I had of a woman dying of cancer — she was riddled with it. I had talked to her about Burrswood, and I said to her "You know I have been receiving the laying-on of hands for you on Thursdays. I haven't told you but I have. Would you like me to go on going up for you and mention your name?" She said "Yes, I would." I went up four weeks running, and I used to go and see her on the Friday after the Thursday, and each time she said "Oh, I feel so much better." She was really helped. I used to say "It will be about five past twelve", so she was very much *there*. One Friday I went in, and she was in tears. I said "What's happened?" and she said "I think I've lost my faith. I didn't get any help yesterday at all." She was deeply upset. I said "This is the most extraordinary thing, because

at the service the regular padre was away, and we had somebody else who got a bit muddled up, and I got left out." That made me feel it was well worthwhile going up for the patients. She was a very matter-of-fact person . . . not at all emotional.

Later, after Dr. Aubert had joined the staff, it became the custom for Dr. Aubert and Dr. Elliott to assist the priest in the laying-on of hands.

Dr. Elliott has, from time to time, felt worried by people's tendency at Burrswood to turn recoveries into 'miracles'.

In medicine there are so many areas of medicine that we don't really know about or understand — and of course, we know that with cancer cases and leukaemias there can be remissions. It is often difficult to know what has really happened, but I don't mind that. So long as the patient is helped, what does it matter?

In his years at Burrswood, Dr. Elliott can remember a number of cases that seemed to him to make inexplicable recoveries, and so might tentatively be described as 'miracles' if one wanted to use the word. Such a one was an American woman who arrived at Burrswood in a very advanced stage of cancer; there were X-rays and biopsies that proved it. She arrived on a stretcher and lay in bed, immobile.

I gave her steroids, which was the first time I had used steroids here. Dorothy worked on her very hard. Everybody thought she was going to die, but gradually she got better, and about a year later she went back to America to her family. Before she went I said to her "Please put in your will that if anything happens to you there'll be a post-mortem to see what has happened", and she agreed. Some years later she slipped and fell and got a disc lesion. They operated in America, and she died under the anaesthetic. There was a post-mortem, and there was evidence only of healed cancer!

* * *

One of the intriguing things about the sudden 'healings' witnessed at Burrswood is that they don't necessarily happen to 'deserving' cases, in the sense of people with a strong faith or conviction. Dr. Elliott remembers one high-ranking army officer with a blood pressure so high that it could not be registered on any machine.

After various attempts to treat him in South Africa he was sent back to England to die. He had led a rakish life and dabbled in black magic. He disliked Burrswood on sight, said it was a ridiculous place and he didn't believe in it, and Dorothy Kerin used to come out of his room saying "It's no good. I can't get anywhere with him." I treated him with up-to-date medication. Suddenly, after about three months he started getting better. At five months his blood pressure was down to a reasonable level. He went back to London, went on living a rakish life and eventually died of a cerebral haemorrhage two years later.

There were other kinds of healing, less dramatic, but infinitely precious to the recipients. A present member of the community who spent years getting over a severe mental breakdown at Burrswood, remembers how, in the warm and loving atmosphere Dorothy Kerin created, it was possible to emerge from the shadows. She did not desire close contact and Dorothy Kerin sensed this in her friendly, accepting way, knowing both how to let her be, and also to give her the feeling that she loved and cared. To someone in a withdrawn state it seemed impressive that Dorothy Kerin took an intense interest in current events; she never let the narrower world of the Burrswood community, with all its cares and preoccupations, enclose her. She was part of the whole human race.

Interestingly, another ex-patient who had suffered a nervous and physical collapse in the Ealing days, also said that she had found this wider vision of Dorothy Kerin's a healing factor.

The mere fact of Dorothy's presence was a tremendous help. If you met her in the passages you used to get a smile or some laughing remark from her. I was very struck how she was so interested in everything that was going on outside. She wasn't, as one might have thought, only interested in the people she was seeing, and the kind of help she was giving. Any unhappiness, or any jubilation in the world outside and she was always in on it. It made a great impression on me because I had given up reading newspapers or listening to the wireless or anything of that kind.

Someone who came to know and admire Dorothy Kerin from a quite different standpoint was Kay Clemetson, a journalist, who was a neighbour to Burrswood. Burrswood drew its water supply (it still does) from a spring which rose in a valley on her property, and she and her husband had arranged a meeting with Dorothy Kerin because the reservoir which belonged to Burrswood looked like bursting its banks and washing away their drive.

I can see her now standing there looking at the little reservoir, and looking at the water seepage over the old drive that ran by. It was getting very dangerous; it was going to wash it right the way down over the edge to the ram below, and we were very worried about it. I remember my husband saying "You see, Miss Kerin, if something isn't done, the whole of this drive will be washed away". And she stood looking at it and quietly said "I don't think it will!" He was a very practical man, and he was exasperated, because he could see it was bound to happen. But she knew it wouldn't. And it didn't!

Kay Clemetson developed a close friendship with Dorothy Kerin, and felt that one of the things she could do for her was sometimes to give her a rest from the busyness of life at Burrswood.

I recall walking with her through the gardens here one day, and from behind all the nooks and shrubs someone would pop out "Oh, Dorothy could I just ask you so-and-so . . . ? Oh, Dorothy!" You couldn't get her away from people here, which was natural, because everybody loved her so much. So I used to steal her and Dorothy Arnold away to come and sit by the log fire in my little home, and we used to have wonderful evenings when Dorothy Arnold and I would get into deep conversations on some topic of spiritual interest to us, and Dorothy Kerin would sit just quietly there looking at the fire, apparently paying no attention. But every now and then she would come out with something that was very relevant, and which meant a great deal. You would think she was paying no attention, but she was.

There were two sides to Dorothy. She had a very human side, a great sense of humour, and she could be exasperating very often with her way of just brushing things off. Then there was the other deep side which you felt very, very much. I felt the depth of her spiritual quality. There was something that was just very, very special about Dorothy.

This combination of human and spiritual qualities made Kay Clemetson feel that she could envisage the sort of personality that Jesus had been. 'She was so *human.*'

Kay Clemetson shared with Dorothy Kerin a great pleasure in the company of dogs, and when her golden labrador bitch fell ill with a paralytic disease which caused her great pain, and which the vet could not cure, Dorothy Kerin surprised her by insisting that she bring her to a healing service. The dog was given the laying-on of hands, and at first showed no sign of responding, but exactly three days later it was suddenly perfectly well with no pain, and no recurrence of the disease. "Interesting" was Dorothy Kerin's comment, when she was told of it. "I've known that three day period before."

A slightly different view of Dorothy Kerin in her early Burrswood days comes from Ted Russell, who, together with his brother Wally, ran a small building business in Groombridge. She asked him to visit her soon after her arrival at Burrswood in order to see to the drains for her, and said that there were other jobs she would like him to do for her. She didn't like big firms, she said. Gradually, he began to undertake repairs for her, then to do extensions to the house, and rebuild the old stables and outhouses.

Like Dr. Elliott, he was conscious that she was a 'woman alone', and this made him want to help her as much as possible. He noticed that she herself was a terrific worker — 'she worked twenty-four hours a day' — but that none of it was for her own prosperity or wellbeing. 'I remember her wearing the same old brown dress till it practically dropped off her!'

Her high spirits were most attractive. 'In the early years she was always gay and laughing, though the work wore her down eventually.' But there was something else to her. 'A *mysterious* woman, that's what I always felt.'

Over the years, Dorothy Kerin and Ted Russell gradually moved into a close working partnership, she with her vision of beauty and the way in which Burrswood must develop, he with the practical craftsman's knowledge and experience to carry it out.

'People talked about her spiritual achievements. I don't know so much about those. But what I admire were her physical achievements. I'm a practical man, and I think that what she managed to get done here in the way of buildings was amazing.'

When she was planning a new project she would say to him "Will you accept a challenge?" When he said yes, she would say "Bring your men along tomorrow, and we will all have a glass of sherry together and talk about it." Then she would say to them "Mr. Russell has accepted the challenge. Will you?" And it usually was a challenge, because she expected everything to be done in the shortest possible time. It was no use asking for extra time to catch up on work, or even to allow work already undertaken to 'settle'. She would simply reply that there wasn't time, that she had a lot of work to get through and only so much time to do it in, and it must be finished.

This placed Ted Russell under a lot of strain at times; he would wake up at three in the morning trying to solve the practical problems she set him, and at one point almost broke under the strain. His wife was enraged at the way Dorothy Kerin worked him. She expected him to work alongside his men, "We all work here. I don't want the sort of boss who walks round in a bowler hat" — but this meant that he spent all his evenings catching up on the paperwork of his business. The men, too, thought her a bit of a driver, and there was a sense in which she was ruthless. She would become very angry if she thought her own ideas were threatened.

And yet she was also a courteous and concerned employer. She saw to their physical comfort — he remembers her in hot, dusty weather, coming out with trays of cold drinks — and she wanted to know if any of them had problems. "If they have problems, they can't work properly." She teased them, and jollied them along, and Ted Russell remembers her saying to his brother who was unevenly sunburned from working in a string vest "You look like a red cabbage in a net!"

He always felt a sinking of the heart, however, whenever she came up with a fresh idea for building, wondering what conundrum she would set him this time. She would say "Now I've got an idea for so-and-so. You go and see the architect and draw up some plans and we'll see. I haven't got the money now, but I'll have it by the end of the month . . ." The Russell auditors warned them about the risks of this method of doing business, but Ted Russell used to reply "I can only say that I trust this woman . . ." His trust in her never turned out to be misplaced.

Among the work Ted Russell and his firm accomplished was a number of chapels built within the house, each one replaced by a larger one as it became unable to accommodate the numbers who came to the healing services, the east wing pulled down and rebuilt, (St. Faith's) a major staircase removed and rebuilt (the Russell brothers said at first that this was impossible, but Dorothy Kerin airily replied that she had 'seen it'), and then the building of Chapel House. Some of these were considerable undertakings for what Russell calls 'two village lads', though they were dwarfed by their even greater achievement in building the church, of which more in the next chapter.

The closeness of their co-operation in these immense labours, gruelling as it often was at the time, means a great deal to Ted Russell in retrospect. He still treasures, and wears, a sheepskin coat Dorothy Kerin gave him one year for Christmas.

4

As Burrswood became thoroughly established, and even better known to people outside its boundaries, Dorothy Kerin became very much in demand both as speaker and as one who would visit the chronically sick in their own homes, talk and listen to them and give them the laying-on of hands. It is not clear how she decided whom she would visit — she must have received many requests for this kind of help, that she neither did, nor could respond to. But much of her work she understood in terms of intercessory prayer — she was in the habit of rising at about four in the morning and spending an hour in prayer before the household was up — and in the light of this decided what action she would take.

Peggy Simpson, who acted as her driver, remembers one immensely long journey they took, under difficult conditions to visit a sick woman in Edinburgh.

> It was winter, and there were terrible reports on the wireless of snow and ice in the north. Jummie said "Dorothy, you *can't* go". Dorothy said "I'm going!" We set off, and were all right till we got to Grantham, when we ran into thick fog and drove through it all through the night. Dorothy's appointment in Edinburgh was at half past eleven, and we got there just on the dot. At five o'clock we set off home again, 460 miles! We did some shopping in Princes Street first. We got to Baldock at about eight and ate a huge breakfast, and when we got to London at about twelve, Dorothy said "I must get one or two things in Peter Jones!" When we got home I went to bed and slept right through till the next morning.
>
> Dorothy was marvellous on a long journey like that. We mostly took our own meals, but on the way back she reckoned always to stop somewhere where we could get out of the car and sit down and have a good meal and real rest for an hour or so.

Night driving, when they were going to distant destinations, proved a useful way of fitting in Dorothy Kerin's many engagements. Peggy preferred it to getting up and setting off in the middle of the night, and Dorothy Kerin was able to sleep on the way and arrive fresh the next morning. She sat in the back, sleeping in an upright position.

They did not often talk to each other on these long trips. Peggy saw them as an opportunity for Dorothy Kerin to relax, and think her own thoughts, away from the tyranny of the telephone and constant callers. 'Sometimes we went all the way to London without saying a word. Unless she spoke to me I never started a conversation, unless it was to do with where we were going.'

They covered around 30,000 miles a year on these car journeys and Peggy remembers trips to Cornwall and Devon, Shrewsbury, Preston, York and Leicester and many more places. On the journey to Cornwall they visited an old priest with cancer, and also a young child with cancer of the liver. Both subsequently died. 'She did a great deal for the parents of that child.' On such a visit she would stay at least half an hour, sometimes longer, but she would never accept an invitation to stay the night, and rarely one to have a meal. She said that it was too difficult for everyone concerned to switch from the spiritual to the social focus.

On overnight journeys she still kept her hour of prayer between four and five in the morning just as she did at home. She would tell Peggy when she was beginning so that she did not speak to her.

A little later Dorothy Kerin extended her travelling to include speaking engagements and taking services. She had neither the time, nor perhaps the need, for long preparations of papers. Existing tapes of talks that she gave follow a particular sort of pattern. They are simple, direct, totally unpretentious. There is never any trace of trying to impress, or be clever, nor is there any false modesty. She spoke straight-forwardly of her belief, of her trust in God, often using biblical quotation, and perhaps nowhere is her conviction that she was a 'little bit of pipe' more compellingly illustrated. There is a curious transparency about her utterances, both spoken and written, as if it really was her desire that her audience should see through her and past her to what it was that she saw. She often described her own youthful healing and the work to which it led, but without a trace of self-importance or dramatics. It was simply a fact.

> After a period of waiting upon God in prayer it was made abundantly clear that God had brought me back to use me in His Name to heal the sick, to give faith to the faithless and comfort the sorrowing. As the years have passed, these commands have been fulfilled, and through the power and goodness of God, we have seen many of those wonderful Acts of the Apostles re-enacted before our eyes: the blind have seen; the lame have walked; the deaf have heard; the faithless have found faith and the sorrowing have been comforted — thanks be to God.
>
> We have come to know that with God — our living God — nothing is impossible, and for those who have eyes to see and ears to hear the message is still true — I am the Lord that healeth thee. His arm is not shortened, His power is no less than in those days two thousand years ago when He walked among us healing all who came to Him.

Peggy Simpson understood Dorothy Kerin's way of preparing herself to speak, not as filling of her mind with ideas, as is the way with most speakers, but just the opposite.

> She would get in the car and after a bit she would say "I haven't a thought in my head about what I shall say." She would so *empty* herself, and then she got up in the pulpit or stood in the chancel and it just poured out. I suppose I took her to between fifty and a hundred different places to speak, and she said that every time, and yet I've never heard her tell her story in the same way twice. It seemed new to me every time. She had a wonderful ability to suit what she said to her audience. There was always a dead silence in the church — you could hear a pin drop. She spoke without hesitation and with such authority.

In her first years as a speaker i.e. in the late forties and early fifties, Dorothy Kerin was not invited to speak from the pulpit — this only began with an invitation from a clergyman in Torquay. She encountered a certain amount of hostility from some clergy, who seemed to resent a woman having things to say on spiritual matters, a resentment which was gradually overcome, and which was, in any case, outweighed by the many priests who admired her work. But she used to say that doctors were much easier to deal with!

Her public appearances were often followed by long sessions with individuals in various kinds of distress, but she had a remarkable capacity to recover from the fatigue and nervous strain that such occasions imposed.

> She would drop it off her shoulders when she got back in the car. When we stopped to have a meal, nobody could have been more fun. You felt she'd just risen — it was as if she was starting the day instead of ending it.
>
> She got pleasure out of the long journeys, particularly if they could drive fast. She loved speed. "Go on, pass it, pass it" she would say, if another car appeared in front of us.
>
> She loved looking at the countryside as we passed. And she loved antique shops. As we passed she would shout "Stop, stop, I must go in there. I've seen something". I remember her saying it half way up that awful bend in Dorchester near Oxford. We bought several things in there — a fireplace, a plinth for a statue, and a cherub. If Dorothy went into what she called a junk shop and saw something that she thought ought to be in the church, she just bought it. Nothing pleased her more than going round a junk shop.
>
> "How much is that?" she would say. "Oh really. Well, let's look at something else." Then she'd go back to it. She always beat them down in the end.

Many of these trips were made in a second-hand upright Daimler, useful for taking the children to school which was also Peggy's job. She had hair-raising journeys while the children fought in the back of the car. She eventually armed herself with a ruler, to maintain order in the back, and to keep them away from the door-handles, but in spite of her vigilance one of them once fell out! Later Peggy drove Dorothy Kerin on the regular visits to the children at their various boarding schools.

She remembers their long journeys together with immense pleasure. 'It was a wonderful time in my life, being able to do that for her. I loved every second of it.' She was struck by the way that, far from being depressed by the suffering she so often witnessed, Dorothy Kerin invariably saw it as part of 'Our Lord's will' and so, ultimately right and endurable. She felt that it was because of this that she was so often able to give real comfort and a sense of hope to people in very extreme kinds of distress.

Throughout the fifties the work of Burrswood continued to grow, and more and more people, particularly in the Churches, began to feel that they must look again at what Dorothy Kerin always referred to as 'Divine healing'. The extreme religious scepticism of the thirties and forties had begun to recede, and a new generation was growing up who, far from finding religious experience embarrassing or intellectually offensive, looked towards it with deep interest and real hunger. Dorothy Arnold has remarked that what brought people to hear Dorothy Kerin was 'an immense hunger for genuine religious experience; all the churches, and they were many, in which she spoke, whatever their denomination, were filled to capacity.' She was speaking of Dorothy Kerin's visit to Sweden in 1959 (though the same would have been true in any other country including Britain). In the late fifties and early sixties Dorothy Kerin began to be in demand by a much larger Christian audience, and to visit, by invitation, Switzerland, France, and America. A Burrswood worker recalls meeting a woman in France who couldn't speak a word of English, but who remembered the occasion on which she heard Dorothy Kerin speak (in English) as one of the transforming events in her life. In addition to these working trips, Dorothy Kerin also had a holiday in Italy, one of the very few she was ever to take; she enjoyed herself immensely and came back laden with treasures which would later decorate the church.

The exhausting working itineraries abroad were an extraordinary undertaking for a woman of seventy, particularly since she had overworked systematically for years. But in addition to this there was the new, and gigantic project of building a church, the Church of Christ the Healer, as it came to be called. She had had a vision of the church being built on the existing rose garden, and at once sent for Ted Russell. He said that it would take three or four years to build what she wanted, and she said that that was nonsense, that she wanted it by the following year. She wanted the church built in stone, and he knew that suitable stone was very expensive, and would take a long while to get. In the end, he hit on a kind of reconstituted stone that was both beautiful and far cheaper than solid stone. In July of 1959 there were still roses growing on the site, when Dorothy Kerin emerged from the house, saying "I've just been talking to the Bishop and he says he'll come on May 14th next year to open the church!"

For Ted Russell, it was to be the beginning of the most exacting of all the many exacting building jobs he did for Dorothy Kerin. He had 16–18 men working on the site, and he and his brother worked alongside them. They worked a twelve to fourteen hour day and went home each night beaten with exhaustion. Yet he remembers it now as the best thing in his whole working life.

'She gave me a wonderful chance to express myself, and I'm grateful to her. Where else would two village lads like Wally and me get the chance to build a church?'

The Church of Christ the Healer is a fine building, of yellow reconstituted stone outside (looking very much like 'Cotswold stone'), painted white inside, with a blue ceiling. It is basically very simple, and makes a good setting for some of its elaborate ornaments. But these are each very fine — there is none of the shoddy rubbish that used to cheapen Catholic and Anglo-Catholic churches — chosen with real feeling for decorative taste. What has been achieved is a church that breaks across barriers of taste and class. Those with untutored aesthetic tastes feel this really *is* a church — there is much there to touch upon conventional religious emotion. Those with more artistic feeling find themselves confronted with a highly individual and fully developed style and taste (this is also true of the houses Dorothy Kerin furnished) and, though, like all highly personal taste, it cannot appeal to everyone there is much that is beautiful and impressive.

The church was dedicated by the Bishop of Coventry on May 14th, 1960, just as Dorothy Kerin had said it would be.

Yet the immense effort that went into inspiring such a major effort together with all her other work, and her taxing journeys abroad, began finally to tell on Dorothy Kerin. Towards the end of 1961 she suffered severe exhaustion, and began to have trouble with her heart. In the spring of 1962 she suffered a heart attack. She was, in fact, to have a number of minor heart attacks — Peggy Simpson remembers the frightful anxiety of watching her have a heart attack in the car on a shopping expedition — and she continued for a year or two to suffer failing health. At Christmas 1962 she was taken seriously ill on Christmas Eve, and she died on January 26th, 1963, easily and instantaneously, while talking to Dr. Aubert.

It was Dr. Aubert who announced her death to a meeting of the Burrswood staff in the chapel, and it was fitting that he should do so, for not only was he her doctor, but he was her chosen successor as Warden of Burrswood. She had met him on a sick visit to Guernsey at a time that he was practising there as a G.P. and had at once been impressed by his quality and suitability for her work. He had joined her at Burrswood in 1962, working alongside her in the partnership of religion and medicine that was her special contribution to the art of healing. Her death was a shattering blow to those who had worked with her, and the many who had been in the habit of turning to her in all the difficulties and vicissitudes of their very difficult work. She was, as one of them put it, 'very much a one-man band', despite the loyalty of her team. But the foundations had been too well built to collapse and, as the next chapter shows, the work continued and flourished.

First, however, the work of Burrswood had to undergo a long and difficult ordeal that continued in various forms for about eight years. When a charismatic leader dies there is always a crisis: can the work continue without them, and if it does, will the memory of the leader help or hinder? Those who loved the leader tend to disagree among themselves about what he or she would have wished, and there is the continuing dilemma of whether to preserve what has been achieved in the past or adapt to new circumstances and opportunities with bold changes. Dr. Aubert, with his quiet manner, his tact, and his own vision and insight, proved to be the ideal pilot for these difficult waters.

But the most painful part of the ordeal was beyond his control. Dorothy Kerin had not left a will, a dispute arose whether her children should inherit her estate, or whether it should remain intact for the continuance of her healing work. Since much of her estate had been accumulated as a result of the wish of others to assist her work, the Burrswood staff felt it should continue to be used for this purpose, whereas Dorothy Kerin's children felt they were entitled to inherit in the usual way. If they had done so, the work would have been totally destroyed. As it was, the legal battle dragged on for years, until in 1969 a settlement was made in which the children received £4,500 each plus legal costs. It had been an anxious time for Burrswood, costly on every level.

But what finally, must be said of Dorothy Kerin? Above all, that she had what might be called a 'therapeutic personality.' People were healed because of her, either directly and immediately, or slowly and with considerable personal struggle. Her touch, or her presence, or her words, or all three, made them feel better, able to rally their own healing resources or to yield to the knowledge that recovery was impossible. She brought about a transformation. As the soldiers said of Florence Nightingale in the terrible wards of Scutari, 'Before she came there was cursing and swearing, but after, it was holy as a church.' Or as Ruth Farr put it, less dramatically, but very convincingly:

> She took away care and fears. I have often wondered how this was accomplished. It had very little to do with what she said, and certainly she did not go in for clichés or platitudes. I think she must have taken people, whether it was apparent

or not, into the orbit of her prayers, into that area where love is, and there fear became lost in a sea of tranquillity.*

Healing ability is not all that rare — we have all known doctors, nurses and therapists of one kind and another who had it to a marked degree. What is rare, and to my mind a kind of genius is to possess it so markedly as Dorothy Kerin or Florence Nightingale, in such concentration that the sick feel better just because you enter the room.

It is not, of course, possible thoroughly to dissect this sort of genius any more than any other kind; one may only uncover strands which seem significant in the whole.

A strand in Dorothy Kerin's character which I think everyone I spoke to referred to without exception was her happiness.

'She was captivating . . . she was the gayest thing . . . she was such fun . . . she was always laughing . . . she used to give the most marvellous parties. We all dressed up and she would come as Marie Antoinette or someone.'

Here was the description of someone who took great joy in living, an impression borne out by the many photographs of her in every one of which she is smiling. Happiness of that kind is, one may guess, rooted in a number of things — a particular sort of confidence and trust in life (very infectious to others), a freedom from anxiety, an unself-consciousness. She herself saw her relationship to life as one of 'obedience'. At the centre of her understanding of the meaning of the world and of human existence was God, and all that was asked, of her or of others, in joy or suffering, in health or sickness, was conformity to His will. This was the unchanging framework in which her whole life was lived, from the day of her miraculous healing when she felt herself called back to life from the borders of death to the day on which she died fifty-one years later. It was in one sense a huge simplification of life which set her enviably free of the conflicts which tear at many of us. It was tremendously costly in terms of fatigue, nervous strain, and freedom to lead a normal life.

What to her was the great consolation in the stresses and

*Ruth Farr, *Will You Go Back?*, The Dorothy Kerin Trust.

deprivations of her life was her relationship to Jesus Christ. From the time of her healing she had felt a growing identification with him, an identification which we may guess became complete at the time of her receiving the Stigmata. Dorothy Arnold's classification of what followed as 'Spiritual Marriage' in the sense in which it is described by St. John of the Cross and other great mystics, seems exactly right. Partly Christ *is* Dorothy Kerin; partly he is 'the other'. It is like a marriage, and it is more than a marriage. When she said that her children were to have God for a father she was saying something that was true for her beyond the usual generalisation about God being the father of all mankind.

This sense of her close relationship to Christ impressed many people, from the most sophisticated to the most simple. Dr. King's and Kay Clemetson's insight, through Dorothy Kerin, of what Jesus must have been like as a person, is matched by that of a small child who came to a party at Burrswood.

'My eldest daughter, who was four, came with me to a party, and Marina took her upstairs to take her coat off. She took her into Dorothy's room. When they came downstairs Gill said "Daddy, I've just been in Jesus' bedroom." She knew nothing about the place, just sensed the extraordinary atmosphere there was about Burrswood.'

It was this sense of relationship to Christ that permeated her whole attitude to healing. Dr. Kenneth Cuming, doctor, priest, and present Warden of Burrswood, remembers his own first encounter with her. As a curate at Bramley in Surrey he had been brought over to visit Dorothy Kerin by a parishioner, who introduced him with some comment about his being a healer. He never forgot what followed.

'She took my hands in hers — I remember how soft and warm and small they were — and looked up at me with very wide-set blue eyes, and said "There are no healers save Christ, but you are a channel. Make sure you're a good one!" And she put my hands together and walked off.'

But although Dorothy Kerin is what I would call a Christian healer through and through it is worth noting that she was within an ancient tradition of healers that goes back to pre-

Christian times to the Greek Aesculapius and his teacher Chrion. Not only does she, as the Greeks did, see healing as a mixture of medical skill and religious ritual (in order, as it were, to 'get right' with oneself and with Divine authority), but like some of their famous physicians she was a 'wounded healer'. She had begun her ministry with a cruel illness, and she was subjected to illness for the rest of her life, though much less so in the latter half of it.

What in the light of this is to be said of Dorothy Kerin's own psychology? There has been an over-defensive tendency among Christians to insist that their spiritual geniuses — the saints, healers, confessors, were free of all neurotic and psychopathic tendencies, without considering that without such wounds (wounds that are almost commonplace in the case of other types of genius) they would have lacked the necessary vision and insight. 'We have come to take it for granted' wrote the pyscho-analyst Erik Erikson, describing the genius of Luther 'that any greatness harbours massive conflict.'*

We can know little at this distance of the 'massive conflict' that shaped Dorothy Kerin, can only link it tentatively to her feelings for the father whose death in early adolescence precipitated a long decline, and guess that her delay in breaking free of the Langford-James's and going out into the world to start her ministry was part of the same conflict. She is not in the slightest diminished by such a speculation; rather we may surmise that out of the unconscious agony that nearly shattered her sprang the inner knowledge of physical and mental suffering that was to be life-giving for hundreds, if not thousands, of fellow men and women.

Someone well acquainted with the outstanding facts of this period, has suggested that in these very facts lay the ingredients of this 'massive conflict'. For example it is known that after her initial refusal to take monastic vows — as her Director wanted her to — Dorothy Kerin was subjected to the most subtle pressures to achieve this end. Finally she gave in gracefully in circumstances that would be prohibited in Religious Orders.

Secondly it is known that she believed, (quite wrongly), that

**Young Man Luther,* Faber.

her Spiritual Director could command obedience of her in ways which were in reality quite untenable.

Release from this situation — whatever the cause of conflict — lent her an extraordinary degree of drive and strength (I do not myself believe that this is in conflict with the statement often made that her superhuman strength and determination came from her relationship with Christ) a strength which made it possible for a woman, helped in the main by other women, to achieve remarkable things, at a time when it was unusual, even eccentric, for women to embark on original enterprises single-handed. It is impossible not to make comparisons with Florence Nightingale, whose conflict also expressed itself in prolonged illness, and who had a profound sense of the religious nature of her vocation. Whereas Florence Nightingale, however, withdrew after the great Scutari *tour de force* into an invalidism which was to deepen throughout her life, Dorothy Kerin found unlooked-for reserves of health and high spirits, which suggests that her problem was partly, if not wholly, resolved.

The only doubts on this subject must come by way of her apparent inability to establish a fully satisfactory relationship with her adolescent children. When no longer pretty and innocent 'babies', children, and particularly adolescent children, often touch upon parental conflict. Reading her various comments about them, one wonders if Dorothy Kerin did not see babies and children as pretty and innocent young animals, like the puppies and kittens she loved so much, rather than, as parents discover, either to their joy or dismay, a devastating confrontation with their own prejudices, ambitions, beliefs, repressions and neuroses. It was perhaps the only area of her life in which Dorothy Kerin would not face confrontation, which aligns her with many parents of lesser calibre.

Perhaps it is part of her longing, so deeply understandable in view of the loneliness and unusualness of her vocation, to be 'ordinary', to be like other people, to enjoy the things ordinary people enjoyed — a home, children, the country, animals. Indeed, a lot of her was ordinary, sharing conventional tastes in furnishing, clothes, education, entertaining. Her uniqueness in other respects must have made her more conventional pursuits (her passion for shopping, particularly in Peter Jones and Selfridges, her children's parties, her country walks, etc.) a real solace, a sheet anchor of sanity in a world which at other times was rocked by the encounter with God and the Devil, with ecstasy and with suffering.

Yet for other people it was her encounter with the mysteries which was precious and life-giving, and it has continued to be so since her death. A few years ago I met a businessman who had come across one of Dorothy Kerin's books and became fascinated by the thought of her. He travelled to Herne Hill to look at the house where she lived as a child, and then went on to Burrswood to meet people she had known. The thought of her became for him a life-giving experience. "I can't get over the feeling that here was a saint actually in our own life-time" he said to me several times. He had, though he didn't know it, only a year or two to live, and in that time became deeply and creatively involved in the life of Burrswood. Ten years or more after her death, Dorothy Kerin's healing touch was still at work, as it will be for many years to come.

PART TWO

Burrswood Today

I

BURRSWOOD IS SET in one of the most beautiful parts of England, in a gentle pastoral landscape which, under certain lights, and at certain times of the year, has the mystical intensity of Samuel Palmer's paintings. The traveller arriving at Burrswood passes through Groombridge, a beautiful and unspoiled village, and enters the long drive up to the house. It winds among trees and small copses, past fields with grazing cattle and a pond, past St. Luke's and the gardens and on to the front door of Burrswood. In the autumn there are hedges covered in blackberries and a breathtaking glory of golden leaves.

Inside the front door there is the atmosphere of an unpretentious country house — that mixture of polished woodwork, worn but good quality carpets, comfortable chintz-covered armchairs and relaxed friendliness that is peculiarly English. The visitor who is not desperately ill, but who has perhaps come for advanced convalescence becomes at once part of the life of the house. He will eat at the enormous round table in the dining-room, finding himself with a deaf old lady on one side of him and a theological student helping out at Burrswood on the other. Afterwards, sitting in the drawing-room, he will talk to a whole range of people — a clergyman getting over a breakdown, a young mother who has had an operation and who is painfully homesick for her children, a middle-aged woman who comes at regular intervals for rest for a severe heart condition, a university lecturer who is wrestling with the knowledge that she has a terminal illness, a titled old lady struggling with arthritis. Visitors are not encouraged to unload the details of their illnesses on one another, yet the burden of worry that many bring with them is not easily laid aside, and sooner or later the painful details slip out.

The regime is quiet and uneventful as in any nursing-home — afternoon rests, early nights, gentle strolls round the garden. But at every point, from the friendly reception to the sympathetic interest of the nurses, from the cheerful way the food is served to the loving way in which it has been cooked, the visitor is made to feel that he matters, that others really care about his fears or his bodily pains, that they care enough to make the house and garden beautiful for him and to organise their working hours around his needs. There is no sense of hurry, no implication that, meal-times apart, he must fit in with their convenience or timetable. If he badly needs a chat and a cup of tea at three o'clock in the morning, then he can have it, and, what is more, have his need attended to as if it is the most normal thing in the world. So that staying at Burrswood is rather like being cared for by a marvellously warm, competent, and loving mother.

The patients who are too sick, on arrival, to join in the life of the house, enjoy an even more meticulous care. Sister Maria, a recent sister in charge, comments that patients are often tense and fearful when they arrive and that the first step in helping them is to enable them to relax. Nervousness can make some patients extraordinarily truculent and difficult, or downright eccentric ('I remember one woman who came with dozens of clothes that took the nurses hours to put away!') But caring for the patient means extreme tolerance to begin with. ('For the first forty-eight hours we let them get away with a lot') but within forty-eight hours most patients *do* begin to relax — a result, Sister Maria feels, of getting a number of details right. She gives a list of what seems to her important at this stage — 'good food, comfort, nice surroundings, the correct medication at the right time, attention to the patient's worries.' Given this kind of reassurance that he is going to be cared for, the patient can begin to devote his energies to getting better.

It is not always easy to find nurses who understand exactly what is required of them at Burrswood — a quiet personal approach that is far removed from the rush and almost mechanical methods of some hospitals, and yet an uncompromising attention to the highest medical standards.

There is a precise balance of physical care and human warmth that is right for patients and which gives them the maximum chance of recovery.

Part of the secret of the good nursing at Burrswood is the right nurse/patient ratio — one nurse to every two and a half patients, or twelve to fourteen nurses to every thirty patients. The number of nurses may be slightly increased if, at any one time, there are a number of 'heavy cases' staying at Burrswood. The nurses get a modest wage, with everything found and about fifty per cent of them are fully trained. It is not altogether easy to find nursing staff, partly because Burrswood is rather 'cut off' geographically for those who do not own a car (something few nurses can afford), partly because those who come to Burrswood sidestep the promotion that would come to them as a result of other sorts of nursing experience. But perhaps because the work demands a particular sort of sacrifice and dedication, Burrswood has a core of nurses who love the place and the special sort of opportunity it offers them.

"You see, this is *real* nursing" one of them said to me. They work a forty-hour week most of the time, get a day and a half off, and, when working 'days', work from eight a.m. to eight thirty p.m. with three hours off during the day.

One of the satisfactory things about nursing at Burrswood is that nurses and doctors work as a team with a sense of equality between them. The doctors have one job, the nurses another, but both are concentrated on a common aim — to help the patient get well.

Daily at Burrswood the doctors and nurses together with Joanna Crane, the remedial therapist, meet to talk about their work. They talk, very specifically, about the progress and welfare of individual patients and what might be done to help, medically, or in other ways.

"A. has had a bad night" says one of the sisters. "He is being kept awake by a persistent cough."

"B. has had a headache for the past twenty-four hours at the base of the skull."

"C (a very old man) has been creating havoc at night time, wandering about the corridors, going into people's rooms and turning on the light. I found him at two o'clock in the morning asleep on the drawing-room floor surrounded by cushions!"

Medical assistance for these various problems is discussed,

and Mrs. Crane is asked to give some instruction in relaxation to a woman patient who is exceptionally tense. Mrs. Crane mentions that another woman patient is distressed because she has not had her hair set for several weeks and relatives are coming to visit her. It is arranged that she will have her hair set.

A new patient has lung cancer, but has been told by his own doctor that he has pneumonia. He is obviously worried about the lack of improvement.

"I'm not getting better" he has remarked to the remedial therapist. One of the sisters reports that he has asked her "Will I ever be able to walk again?" "There's a possibility" she has replied. These two conversations suggest that he is deeply worried about his condition, and suspects that he has not been told the truth. Burrswood is against lying to patients, while knowing that not all can bear the truth. (But Sister Maria has previously remarked "Patients don't hear what they cannot bear to hear.")

The next day a Miss C. is arriving with bad arthritis. Is it possible to arrange a room on the ground floor for her?

It is possible to regard some of the details of this conversation as tiny, even trivial, yet seen within the context of enabling the patient to relax and so to concentrate on getting well, they become supremely important. The patient's point of view is an essential part of the sort of medicine practised at Burrswood.

Joanna Crane, the remedial therapist, is a key member of the team. She is at pains to explain that she has built up a method of her own based on an education which began with the social sciences, and moved on to a long training in movement from a gifted teacher who taught, among other sorts of movement, stage movement at the R.A.D.A. She worked at mental hospitals, and then with mentally subnormal children, and found that with a regime of exercises, including breathing exercises, and a therapy that involved the use of colour and music, she was able to get a response from them that surpassed anyone's expectations. With this experience behind her she was fully established in the remedial field, and she was invited to run the medical department of the Horder Arthritic Centre. There, working with severely crippled adults, she found that a whole programme of mental and creative re-education was needed before it was possible to embark on the physical problems of arthritis.

> 'You've got to get people thinking for themselves. If a person is very handicapped, in a lot of pain, sitting in a chair and their hair drops into their eyes, it's an awfully painful thing to get the arm to move to push the hair away. If they have a relative who's kind, and feels sorry for them, he will automatically push the hair out of their eyes, so that in the end they don't think about doing things for themselves. Other people do it for them. Have that happen for many years and they become very self-centred — chronic disease makes you so in some cases, without your being aware of it. But even if you can't walk, there's no need for this. A man's still a whole element, even though he has an incapable body. Inside there's something — a spark — which wants to be able to do things, but it's too darned hard to try, so patients find every excuse they can. The therapist has to fan the spark, make the person *want* to use his faculties again. And that's not easy.'

Methods used were finding the interests of individual patients and helping them to pursue them, on however small a scale — for example, taking a girl who was interested in clothes and fabric design but who was too crippled to sew, to the shop to choose her own materials, rather than letting others choose for her. Painting, choosing things to eat, techniques designed to help patients perform the activities they wanted to perform within their group discussions, exercises performed to music, relaxation — all were aimed at seeing the patient as a whole person.

> You don't function just on a physical level: your physical body is merely the vehicle for your faculties. If the physical body is maimed and maybe the prognosis is poor — maybe you have a condition which will kill you, or maybe it will let you live a long time and you will get more and more crippled

and in pain — you are still a whole faculty, a whole person behind that.

It was happenings like that that decided me to come here — I realised that I knew absolutely nothing about healing and the spiritual qualities it needed. In medicine as it is today we haven't *touched* the healing faculty — the layer in man that is self-healing. Using it is an art that's been lost. Strange awarenesses of this came to me sometimes when I was taking relaxation classes — extraordinary things happened — and I had no one with whom I could discuss it. Then by a strange coincidence I found myself in the grounds here one day — I knew nothing about the place, and within a year I came here to work.

I've learned so much in the bones of this place. We work as a team, right through from the washers-up upwards, or downwards. When patients come here and are helped, consciously or unconsciously, to integrate the bits and pieces which constitute a whole human being, and are not just treated as a physical being, then they are being helped with the process called healing.

Sometimes Joanna Crane sees patients at Burrswood because they have been ordered to have remedial help, sometimes she treats a patient with a terminal disease who needs help with pain.

'If you are afraid of pain, and produce tension, you produce twice the amount of pain. I use breathing to relax their faculties and help them to cope. It's a matter of making the best of the body rather than the worst of it.'

Patients with emotional problems are often helped by painting therapy. Mrs. Crane also gives massage, but will not use any techniques such as diathermy, which depend on machinery rather than human contact.

'I don't think electricity can compensate for manual work. You've lost the individual rapport which is part of the healing element.'

Touching a patient opens the way to a particular sort of understanding.

'A person is particularly vulnerable when he is letting you see the part that hurts most.'

Much of her work is devoted to trying to teach people to live in relaxation rather than tension.

'We deal here with a lot of backs. People have often had a weak back in the beginning or an injury, but they've lived at such a pace and in such a state of tension to keep going that they've harmed it, and you can't replace a back. The answer is to learn how to live. It is similar to chronic arthritis in that way; it's only a difference of degree.'

Joanna Crane recalls how in Greek civilisation, religion, medicine, and art went hand in hand. 'Until you've got that again in a civilisation how can you be whole? You can't. Maybe that's a little bit of what's being begun here.'

2

After Dorothy Kerin herself, the person who was the principal architect of Burrswood was Edward Aubert. Before his death in 1974, when he was Warden of Burrswood, I spent a number of hours with him discussing the work of Burrswood and the hopes he had for it.

Dr. Aubert talked of Burrswood as a medical and spiritual intensive care unit. Good medicine was practised, as good as a dedicated team of doctors and nurses could make it, yet there was belief in spiritual or divine healing. That, he was at pains to explain, did not necessarily mean healing by purely spiritual means, but rather a recognition that all healing came from a Divine source. Burrswood was to aim at the healing of body, mind, and soul, thus attempting something rather different from much medicine practised elsewhere in our day which places all its emphasis on physical healing. Yet Burrswood was not to despise the physical; the defence mechanism and reparative resources of the human body are extremely satisfactory, in themselves a kind of miracle. It is a matter of encouraging them to work as well as possible, and of making use of everything that assists them. We live in a natural world that promotes the process of healing, a world that contains herbs and medicinal salts beneficial to man.

Dr. Aubert did not believe that the technology of the doctor could be insulated from his beliefs. It was an illusion to suppose that technology could be neutral; everything the doctor did or said to the patient illustrated his philosophy of life. The technology of Burrswood was based on a belief in man as the child of God, and was an extension of Dorothy Kerin's aim to heal the sick, comfort the sorrowing, and give faith to the faithless.

Much ill-health, Dr. Aubert believed, was due to a lack of basic trust in life. The negative emotions which sprang from this lack — fear, embarrassment, anger, excitement, and more long-standing ones such as resentment, jealousy, bitterness and self-pity — often seemed to play a key part in illness, though it was difficult always to prove a consistent relationship between illness and emotion. However, by paying attention to the emotional problems of patients as well as to their physical expression, it was often possible to get striking results. Dr. Aubert remembered one patient whose arthritic condition improved amazingly once a lesbian problem was recognised and discussed.

Talking of the effect of the emotions on a T.V. programme he spoke like this:

> Disturbed emotions are at the root of much illness. We talk about people being sick with worry, burning with resentment, being eaten up with self-pity. If these emotions are present in a person, they have to be helped to see that they are there. So that they can be defused. This is partly a psychological task and partly a spiritual task. The psychiatrist helps his patient to come to terms with life in a social context. The spiritual counsellor helps the sick person to come to terms with spiritual realities. As a great deal of real insecurity and fear are due to the fact that the sick person doesn't really know what life is about, cannot see that it has meaning and purpose, we come right up against the importance of spiritual realities. And in many instances part of the therapy is to help the sick person to come to terms with the world of spiritual values and realities and with the ultimate spiritual reality which we call God.*

Just as important to health as the emotions are habits acquired by the patient, and habits are an expression of the patient's beliefs (though seldom deliberately or consciously). Eating too much, drinking or smoking too much, a continual sense of hurry, a need to overwork, all say something about what the patient believes, about himself, or about the world in which he lives. It was, Dr. Aubert believed, often profitable for the patient if he could unearth the belief on which his destructive habits were founded.

One of the recurring problems of sickness was self-pity, which, by riveting the patient's attention to his own suffering or dis-

*'Faces of Christ', B.B.C. television.

comfort, made him feel much worse. A re-education of the attitude of the patient was needed.

Very sick patients needed particular forms of help. Extreme pain and vomiting were nowadays usually controllable by the skilful use of drugs. An important part of caring for the very ill was learning how to ease fear, since this makes an enormous difference to the degree of pain suffered. The knowledge that their pain would get no worse helped a lot of people with terminal illnesses. They also needed help with the thought of death itself. Some were greatly helped by the knowledge that few people die in terrible agony; the end of life is much more often experienced in a floating, semi-conscious state of mind. Other patients wanted reassurance of an after-life and were much helped by the biblical references to life after death and by evidence which points to individual survival.

Asked about failures during his time at Burrswood, Dr. Aubert said that of all forms of illness they had found hysteria the most intractable, though there were sudden breakthroughs into insight and healing.

But the way to care for all patients was basically the same, and Burrswood aimed at the following method:

(a) Accept all patients just as they are, without passing judgment on them and with compassion for whatever they suffer.

(b) Listen to what patients are trying to say. This was one of the most important practices of all, and it broke down into a number of skills. A good listener must

(1) Reduce interruptions to a minimum.

(2) Have a capacity to understand, and to empathise with the problem.

(3) Have compassion.

(4) Have knowledge of life.

(5) Have a capacity for involvement. One of the paradoxes of the medical profession was that often the most gratitude was felt by the patients helped least, just because the doctor devoted more time and worry to them.

(6) Have an open and loving attitude to life.

(7) Have a sense of timing and an ability to recognise genuine distress when he saw it.

(c) Treat patients medically with as much skill as possible and make them as well as possible.
(d) Take into account fears, habits and emotions.
(e) Be prayed for. It was important to Burrswood and its doctors and nurses that their work was enfolded by prayer, and that within the context of prayer they saw their work of healing as a realisation of the will of God.
(f) Use any spiritual resources which are of help to patients e.g. the laying-on of hands, healing services, confession and absolution, anointing, Holy Communion, intercession. By such means patients (who had not been substantially helped by medical treatment alone) were often reached and helped.

The sense of conforming to the will of God could help some patients immensely, taking away the longing for sudden, miraculous release from a trying illness or disability and replacing it with a quiet acceptance. Dr. Aubert quoted the prayer 'Lord, it matters not to me whether I live or die, so long as your will be done.'

A healing capacity, in his view, was a gift which many people had, exactly as they had other gifts and abilities, and one which was capable of many different kinds of development. Some people refused to develop it at all, either from indifference, or because it felt somehow 'eerie' to them. Others chose to develop it as *their* gift, and a number who had enjoyed a popular following were of this kind. Others yet again chose to develop the gift sacramentally, or 'charismatically', conscious of themselves rather as 'acted through' — the channel, or 'bit of pipe' of which Dorothy Kerin spoke — rather than as an agent themselves.

Dr. Aubert was the first of the doctors at Burrswood to give the laying-on of hands. A number of his patients had told him that they experienced relief when he touched them, and this, and the way Burrswood emphasized the partnership of religion and medicine, led to a situation in which he, as well as the chaplain, played this key part in Burrswood's healing services. He also used it privately, and was struck, not only by its healing uses, but by the way in which it could help those afraid to die. He remembered visiting a woman in a nursing home at Tunbridge Wells at the request of a friend of hers. She was dying of cancer, and told that she had six months to live. He tried to ease her fears about dying, and gave her the laying-on of hands. She died two days later. In this, and other cases, there was the impression that in some desperately ill or terminal cases, the laying-on of hands can release a patient so that they can die without fear.

A different kind of release was needed for patients who felt themselves in the grip of some kind of evil possession. Dorothy Kerin's method with such patients had been to work on the building up of their personalities, rather than the expelling of the possessive force. There was, Edward Aubert believed, a real danger in such cases of making the patient's last state worse than the first, or of the possession spreading to the person who tried to help. He quoted one case of a priest, a non-smoker, who tried to help a girl who smoked compulsively by giving her the laying-on of hands. He was entirely successful in curing her, but woke up in the night with such a strong compulsion to smoke that he had to dress and go out and buy cigarettes from a slot machine. The desire to smoke became so permanent and irresistible that he himself had to seek cure by the laying-on of hands.

Dr. Kenneth Cuming, priest and doctor, who is Dr. Aubert's successor as Warden of Burrswood, and who is also Chaplain, has similar remarkable stories to tell of the effect of the laying-on of hands.

> There was a lady who came here to a healing service and asked to see me afterwards. I noticed she was very well turned out, and had a good carriage, and discovered she was a model. She had a lot of pain in her back in the lumbar region. We had a talk about her problem, and I gave her the name and address of a very good, medically qualified osteopath, one of the leading men in the country in

this field. Then she asked me if I would give her the laying-on of hands separately in the little oratory here. I agreed to do this. We went into the oratory and she knelt down. After prayer I put one hand on her head, as we usually do, and the other on her back in the place where she had most pain. After a few minutes she began to wriggle slightly uncomfortably, and I thought perhaps she was finding kneeling difficult with her back, and I had the impulse to stop, so I did so. She rose from her knees with a slightly wry smile on her face and said "Do you normally burn your patients?" I said that I wasn't aware of it, and she said that there was such tremendous heat that she felt she must ask me to stop.

She went her way and I did not see her again till about three months later, when I asked her what the osteopath had said. She said that there had been no need, the trouble had cleared up.

Such effects of the laying-on of hands are not, in Dr. Cuming's view unusual.

'It may be that there is a charismatic energy which flows through those who have the gift of healing, and the patient is, as it were, the resistance, rather as the patient between two electrodes in short-wave diathermy hots up in the middle.'

Dr. Cuming came to work at Burrswood with the feeling that here was perhaps the only place in the country where he could fulfil his dual ministry of priest and doctor. At his first meeting with Dorothy Kerin he had not dreamed that he would come permanently to Burrswood, but he was deeply impressed by the sense of what he calls her 'knowledge', or 'spiritual directness'.

'All spiritually great people have the gift, as Christ himself did, of "knowing what is in men's hearts". They don't waste words on unnecessary chitchat; they just get straight to the heart of the matter.'

By a series of apparent coincidences, which later no longer seemed a coincidence, he came to Burrswood. The first link in the chain was a letter he wrote to Fr. Geoffrey Curtis after seeing him talk in a television programme about life after death. Later they met and Fr. Curtis involved him as a speaker in a conference at which he was to meet Dr. Aubert and others from Burrswood. Dr. Aubert invited him to Burrswood with a view to his becoming Assistant Chaplain.

Dr. Cuming had been Chairman of the Church's Fellowship of Psychical and Spiritual Studies before coming to Burrswood, a body whose function was to help bring back into the Church an understanding of the gifts of the Spirit, and he found the opportunities Burrswood gave him to examine and partake in the gift of healing a very valuable one.

Like Dr. Aubert, he sees the healing power in terms of energy. 'You can use the term spiritual energy if you like. It is an energy many people have to some degree. Those who have a gift of healing are channels for a great power which pours through them. Some people are conscious of it. Some are not. The channel may not feel the power coming through his body or his hands, but the recipient may.'

Dr. Cuming believes that faith, in the sense of a state of trustful expectancy, and what he calls 'affirmative prayer' can be of the greatest importance in healing. 'Negative thought force' on the other hand, a sceptical attitude to the possibility of healing, can impede it; Christ himself could not heal where there was no belief in his powers. Affirmative prayer starts off from the opposite premise that the power is there.

Yet it must be said that the ministry of healing is full of the most baffling contradictions and paradoxes. There are people who seem to have enormous faith and are not healed, and others who appear to have no faith at all and yet are healed.

What must always be considered when thinking about this is that healing is not always of the body, though some critics would perhaps deny there is any other kind of healing. But often because of the power of the mind or the personality or the soul, over the body there are blocks in belief, inner resistances to healing, and these often have to be overcome first before the body can respond. We don't understand the nature of the psychosomatic response. All we know is that it is there and there's a lot of evidence that psychosomatic response does take place. Often when there is a healing of attitudes of mind — a very important part of the healing ministry — then the body begins to respond.

I've known examples — in, for example, a family situation where one of the family has multiple sclerosis — where healing has gradually improved the family situation and made it more tolerable, and then as the family responds, the patient responds. Even though there may be no physical cure at that stage, there is a spiritual cure of relationship. And then you often find that the patient's condition improves. I don't wish to make dramatic claims for the ministry of healing, but I do claim there is often great benefit. And where there is apparent failure, it often seems that there is a reluctance to accept all that is implied in healing; patients simply want relief of symptoms, relief from pain and so on.

However, it must also be said that some people cannot begin to make any spiritual progress whatsoever until their body is healed, or at least their bodily condition — their aches and pains — is ameliorated. Then sometimes the relief is so great that the spiritual healing begins. Until that point is reached there is a total block in any ability to perceive anything beyond it. Pain can be so intense that it blocks everything else; it totally occupies the mind. In such cases one can make religious noises and talk Christian language until one's blue in the face and it's a complete waste of time.

Dr. Cuming feels that the loss of the sense of transcendence, of the numinous, from our churches, has gradually filled people with a longing to experience the reality of God for themselves. The ministry of healing, which could be described as the love of God in action, often helps them a great deal in this search for experience. Healing in this sense often can and does change people's lives dramatically. They are often desperately in need of love, and when they see that love comes in this way it is a most transforming experience. It often has to be gradual. Miracles are not necessarily things which happen overnight in a flash. For many they have to take place in stages, so as not to be too overwhelming for the personality. If they take place in stages, there can be a gradual growth of the soul. One of the problems that arises with the sudden, melodramatic healings that take place at revivalist meetings or at some other healing sessions is 'Can the person healed hold on to what has been given?'

The classic story that is often quoted is of the man healed suddenly of some form of arthritis who threw away his crutches, came down from the platform amid rounds of applause and then was instantly seized upon by the reporters. For a week or so he was the centre of tremendous interest. But after a week or so at home his wife said 'Dear, do you think you feel well enough to cut the grass this morning? Or help with the washing-up, dear? Or do a little shopping for me, dear? And what about a job, dear?"

He was no longer the centre of sympathy and attention and waited on hand and foot. So "A little ache in my shoulder this morning, dear! My leg's feeling stiff" and so on. And within a few weeks he was back on his crutches again.

The story of the Pool of Bethesda illustrates an important aspect of healing. 'Wilt thou be made whole?' (Do you really want to be healed?) All the ingredients of healing are vividly portrayed in the gospels. Being healed can involve giving up things one does not want to give up, a way of thinking about oneself, a way of inviting help from others, or old personality problems left over from childhood.

Dr. Cuming quotes the story of the man in the life beyond who took over with him a problem symbolised by a little red dragon on his shoulder. An angel came to him and said "Won't you let me relieve you of the burden of the little red dragon?" The little red dragon whispered in the man's ear "You can't get rid of me and you can't do without me! You are a part of me and I am a part of you." The man had realised that his whole earthly life had been literally bedevilled by the dragon, so with a despairing cry he said to the angel "For God's sake take him before I want him back." Whereupon the angel put out his hand and took the little red dragon at which there was a magic transformation scene, the little red dragon was changed miraculously into a magnificent white stallion, and the man jumped on the horse's back and away they went. Man and stallion were as one. The story symbolises the centaur, the human and animal nature of man becoming a whole, spirit and sensuality working in harmony.

Dr. Cuming speaks of Plato's analogy of the soul as being driven in a chariot (the body) by the three horses of the mind, the will, and the emotions, with the personality acting as charioteer. The extent to which the charioteer controls the three horses and keeps them in balance enables the soul to fulfil the purpose of the journey. If he fails the soul may be left grieving. Part of contemporary suffering seems to come from denying the existence of the soul in the chariot or even throwing it out altogether.

Some souls seem to need to undergo the experience of suffering in order that more profound spiritual lessons may be learned, and in such cases there may be an unconscious choice of illness as a way of growth. Which is not the same thing as masochistic suffering which can be a destructive and sterile way of dealing with guilt. The conditioned guilt which springs from wrong training in childhood, over-religious training of the wrong kind, whereby God is depicted as a sadistic and angry God, produces a narrow bigotry which produces great suffering for their adherents or for those who oppose them. This kind of suffering is destructive and sterile.

Central to the work of Burrswood is the work of prayer. Dr. Cuming sees this as a kind of enabling process to bring about good things. He says that there are four answers to prayer — yes, no, not yet, or not the way you want it. But where men pray for something that is good, he sees this as a setting to work of the hierarchy of spirits and holy souls, a work which men upon earth often experience as a chain of what appear to be remarkable coincidences. He quotes William Temple — 'When I pray coincidences happen . . . when I don't, they don't.'

3

A THRIVING COMMUNITY and institution like Burrswood cannot exist and cope efficiently with its many-sided work without an effective structure. The final responsibility for the path Burrswood follows rests with the Board of Trustees, a body of eight, which meets four times a year. The members include experts in the field of medicine, religion, social work, business and management. The chairman is Bishop Cuthbert Bardsley, who has been a long-standing friend of Burrswood and of Dorothy Kerin. In broad outline their brief is to see that Burrswood carries out Dorothy Kerin's three-fold task of healing the sick, comforting the sorrowing, and bringing faith to the faithless.

Working beneath the Board of Trustees is the Council, with the Warden as chairman, which meets monthly. This is essentially a management committee, which exists to put policy into effect. Members include at least three members of the Board of Trustees.

There are other Committees — the House Committee which exists to handle essentially practical problems to do with the day-to-day running of the house and gardens, and problems of staffing, catering etc., and the Bookings Committee which considers all cases for admission, bearing in mind the patients medical report, nursing requirements and Bursary assistance in needy cases.

Specialist Committees are set up as the need arises. For example, in 1972, a Teaching Unit Planning Committee examined ways of disseminating knowledge and experience gained at Burrswood. Whilst no teaching unit has yet come about, Seminars are held from time to time for interested groups.

In 1973 another Committee was set up to see how far special provision might be made for sick children at Burrswood. Since the end of 1974 there has been a trial scheme in the main nursing home in which sick children, many of them suffering from leukaemia or spina bifida, and their families, are accommodated. During the first year seventy-two families were accommodated at a cost of £7,300 which was made possible by a three year grant from Joseph Rank Benevolent Trust and some other gifts.

Rising inflation has, of course, hit Burrswood as it has hit all institutions, but it will not bring all expansion to a halt. A well-known architect has recently carried out a study of the Nursing Home complex, and as a result a number of alterations and improvements will be set in hand. There is a need for a reception centre for outside visitors who come to the healing services (around 15,000 a year at the moment) which will keep this side of Burrswood's work separate from the work of the nursing home, and provide the welcoming and interviewing facilities visitors often require. There are also plans to improve the facilities and services of the nursing home.

Burrswood's income comes from a variety of sources, about sixty-two per cent from fees from the nursing home, twenty-five per cent from charitable sources (gifts, donations, offertory, bursary fund and markets) and thirteen per cent from other sources (sales of books, investment income, etc.). There are also legacies which are regarded as capital funds. Since the rapid rise in inflation, it is remarkable that the gifts and legacies have risen to meet it, so that Burrswood's income has increased in relation to rising costs.

By no means all of the sick who come to Burrswood can meet the full fees (these compare favourably with those of any good nursing home) — at any one time the number of patients paying full fees may be between forty per cent and ninety per cent, but the bursary fund exists to help in this way. In 1975, for example, bursary awards (including those to sick children and their families) amounted to £24,000, which meant that one in four patients came to Burrswood at no cost to themselves. The Bursary Fund, however, is never adequate to cover the bursaries, and has to be augmented from charitable income.

Finally, a welcome source of income is the Burrswood Fellowship, though this exists primarily as a fellowship of prayer and moral support. Subscriptions to the Fellowship bring in more than four thousand pounds a year.

Those who carry the burden of Burrswood's work are the staff. This has increased from a devoted handful of Miss Kerin's friends and helpers to a paid staff of around fifty, plus a number of other voluntary helpers. Some of the staff are members of the same devoted group who started Burrswood. Bocky Caudwell is still in charge of the cooking, Marina Chavchavadze visits patients as well as undertaking speaking engagements and a number of outside commissions for Burrswood. Ruth Farr takes care of maintenance and repairs. Johanna Ernest is Bursar. Gwen Williams was, until recently, in charge of intercessions for the Fellowship. Dorothy Arnold, endowed with some of the wisdom and mystical insight of her namesake, is the still centre of Burrswood, to whom many come for advice.

It is only in recent years that Burrswood has appointed an Administrator (at present Michael Selby) to take some of the burdens off the Warden's shoulders, so that he is free of practical details and able to concentrate on the essence of his job — the physical and spiritual care of patients — and the many extensions of this; talking to people who come in search of help, taking part in healing services, keeping abreast of current ways of thought outside Burrswood, receiving guests, choosing staff to fill responsible positions, and, perhaps most important of all, keeping in touch with all the nuances of life within Burrswood from staff morale to the wellbeing of patients. Of first assistance in this are the chaplain and Dr. Elliott and his partners who visit the Nursing Home daily. Dr. King also visits one day a week.

Apart from senior medical and nursing staff, and the band of 'regulars' to whom Burrswood is home, there is something of a staffing problem just because the place is in the country and not very accessible except by car but most institutions suffer in this way. The Australian branch of the Fellowship has encouraged nurses from Australia and New Zealand to come to Burrswood, where they enjoy a very high reputation. Scandinavian nurses and kitchen staff have also been very valuable, a long-term effect of Dorothy Kerin's impact in Sweden, but the government scale on which Scandinavians must be paid makes their services more expensive than those of native staff. Some staff are working at Burrswood as part of their healing process, a half-way house back to ordinary employment. In addition to indoor staff, the place has three full-time gardeners, and one part-time gardener.

A newer and younger member of the staff was Howard who until recently ran a craft shop at Burrswood, and who had a strong sense of the importance of the place.

Burrswood to me is the peak of thirteen years of searching, of trying to find, I suppose you would say, myself. I was in television until 1959, and church affairs or anything even remotely connected with the work here played no part in my life whatsoever. I had a successful life — I don't think it was a particularly happy one. I felt very empty, and when I was about thirty I thought "You've got to take stock of yourself a bit", and for nine months I didn't work. I chucked television and just drifted around London. I thought and thought and tried to find a way out. I can only say that about half way through this nine months a voice, my inner voice I expect, told me very very clearly indeed that I had to go to a community. I had no real idea what a community was, but the voice pestered and pestered me and wouldn't let me go, so eventually in desperation I began to talk to one or two priests about it. Eventually I talked to Kenneth Ross, at All Saints, Margaret Street, and he recommended me to the Franciscans in Dorset.

Howard spent about three and a half months with the Franciscans and nearly became a Franciscan but felt himself pushed on by the voice inside.

So for thirteen years I have worked in different communities. In one I worked, and shared a room with alcoholics and tramps — that knocked a lot of spots off me — and I worked with retarded children, and did a spell of geriatric nursing. Each episode seemed completely disjointed — there was no particular link between any — but looking back now I can see how immensely important all those little episodes were. My basic gifts have always been anything to do with craft or handwork which I studied earlier on. The only time I stepped out of a community during these thirteen years was to be Assistant Curator of an Art and Craft Gallery in Berkshire which I thoroughly enjoyed.

But all the time I became more and more interested in healing. Before I came here I worked at another healing centre in Berkshire. Finally, I spent a weekend with some friends and by chance read some of the books about Burrswood that happened to be there. I had never heard of the place, though for a long time I worked only eight and a half miles away. I thought I must go and see it, and came down for an interview, and when I came I knew that I had to come here. I had to wait quite a long time before I was sure that I could come because Dr. Aubert was away in Canada and I had to wait for him to come back. I kept feeling I should get another job and plough on with something else, but something told me I had to hang on. So I did come. And I can see now that that was the 'jelling' of all the other things I tried to do.

Howard saw one of the problems of living at Burrswood as an insidious insularity. 'One had to be awfully careful not to become Burrswood-bound. It was so easy to do. When I had a day off, I was off like a shot.'

He felt that he learned and re-learned the meaning and value of Burrswood from contact with the patients.

I think what they find is what I found when I first came. It is terribly hard to hold on to that, when you're working there all the time, but contact with the patients teaches you just how great the place is, and what a good future it has. Miss Kerin built the remarkable foundation, but I think it *is* only a foundation, on which they've got a hell of a struggle to build something. It has been a painful path, to move forward, not to stand still, nor to look back to the past, and it has been particularly painful for some of those who worked all their lives to build the place and without whom it would not exist. But if one isn't prepared to go forward like that then you're as good as lost.

Howard sees an ever-widening circle of people as being attracted to Burrswood, not all of whom are accustomed to, or at ease with conventional Christian language. Yet on the other hand he sees Dorothy Kerin's influence as continuing to be central to the thinking and working of Burrswood.

'I never knew Miss Kerin, yet I am terribly conscious of her a lot of the time. I am sure she is still very much about. I think we will be very much aware of her all the time whatever we may do.'

Beyond the community or family of Burrswood there is the wider community of the Burrswood Fellowship, praying for its work, helping it financially, taking an interest in its struggles and developments. An important part of the work of the Fellowship is making, and keeping, the prayer-list. Every day, at the rate of one hundred requests a week, or five thousand two hundred requests a year, the Fellowship Secretary receives letters asking for prayers for people in mental or physical distress, people awaiting an operation, or trying to make some difficult decision, or learning to live with disease or the knowledge of an early death. These names are copied out on to a list and placed upon the altar in the church where their owners are prayed for daily. They remain on the list for a year, except in cases of slow but serious disease where they may remain even if no one has specially requested their inclusion. The Secretary also copies the name, with surname, address and any details about the person prayed for, into a notebook where she can record later developments, healing or death. These books are a moving record of human struggle against heartbreak and pain.

Gwen Williams, for many years the Fellowship Secretary, recalls some of the prayers she has recorded, as she glances through her notebooks.

This one was for a boy who came over here from Australia on a school exchange and developed cancer while he was here. Aged 18. I was asked to put him on the altar because he'd had a setback after a big operation for lung cancer. He then went back to Australia with very little hope that he would live. There was a sudden improvement which continued for a while. But he died quite soon after.

In this one prayers were asked for a man who had had a leg amputated. He made quite a good recovery. People are often very much helped by prayers before an operation because they have such very great fears . . .

This one wrote to give thanks for having made great strides mentally and physically.

This one from a priest who wrote to give thanks for healing from diabetes.

This one about a girl, deeply depressed at the age of 17 who needs freedom from fear.

Gwen Williams sees the act of intercession as a 'lifting up' of the person concerned to God. It is rarely possible to assert definitely that prayer did make a difference in any particular case, if only because so many people — family, friends, doctors, nurses, even schools, can all play a part in 'making whole'.

I remember a little girl whose grandmother brought her to a healing service when she was about four. She couldn't speak, and they had diagnosed some form of spastic handicap. We persevered with prayer, and she came again recently. She is now thirteen and to all intents and purposes perfectly normal. But of course, she has had enormous help from doctors, and from a special school.

Another child prayed for was so backward that she could not attend a normal school. Gradually the child improved, and eventually was able to receive a normal education, but once again she had received enormous help from teachers at her special school.

A more striking account of the possible effect of prayer concerned a man who was dying of cancer, but who refused to accept the fact that he was dying, or to make any arrangements to help his dependents.

He was furious and said that he refused to die, to the great distress of his wife and son. At the request of a local priest we put his name on the list. About two weeks later the priest rang me up and said that an amazing change had come over the patient. He had become reconciled to the thought of dying, was happy, and had made a will to help his dependents. The atmosphere of the whole house had changed. The interesting thing in this case was that the priest had not told the family they were being prayed for and the change of heart had seemed to occur spontaneously.

One of the odd things that has struck Gwen Williams in her years doing the prayer lists is that it is not always those who claim to have enormous amounts of faith who are healed. Some seem to use their faith as a sort of bludgeon.

"I have so much faith that I *must* be healed." But it does not usually work that way.

Prayer, and the healing services, bring extraordinary comfort and help to many who are faced with near-intolerable pain. Rosemary, the mother of four children, told me how, four years previously, she had learned that her seventeen-year-old son had leukaemia and had only a short time to live.

I was a nominal Christian at the time. I believed in Christ, but not in the Church or anything like that. I was completely bewildered, everything was unreal. I had to go to the South of England Show as a judge, and on the way back we got lost and ended up, of all places, in Groombridge. I saw Burrswood and said to my husband "Oh that's where Dorothy Kerin was." I rang them up the next day and they suggested that I came over and had the laying-on of hands by proxy for my son. I had the laying-on of hands, and stood in the church in floods of tears. It all seemed a very faint hope. Then about two nights later I was praying, and had the sensation so many people describe of being filled with light and peace, and from then on the whole thing was transformed. My son had a very long, very protracted illness, with many miraculous happenings. With drugs he had a year's remission and got his A-levels, and then he had his first really serious illness, during which he told me he had become a Christian. Not because he thought he was dying; he was naturally very optimistic. During this first illness he was in terrible pain — such pain that no drugs could alleviate it at all. He was having morphine every three hours, but screaming in pain endlessly and often unconscious. The pathologist at the hospital rang up and said either he must have a complete blood change or there was no hope for him. We felt he had suffered enough and might as well die quickly, so we refused, but then after he had the laying-on of hands he got much better . . . and better . . . and better, and eventually went back to college with virtually no drugs. An odd thing that happened when he was so ill was that he woke up one night and said to my husband, who was sitting by him, "Pa, will you read me the last verse of Thessalonians?" We didn't have a Bible in the house in those days and had to go and find one. The quotation was 'the grace and peace of the Lord Jesus Christ be with you.' But in the morning he said he didn't even know that there was a book of Thessalonians.

For six months he was fine — the specialist said that he would tentatively put forward the word 'miraculous', and of course, I thought it was miraculous — and we had a marvellously happy time, very social with lots of parties. He was full of *joie de vivre*, made lots of friends, and was so natural and normal and jolly. We then had a year during which, every now and then, he would have a terrific illness. Again and again the doctor came and said "I'm afraid this is the end." Every time I rang up Burrswood and they prayed and he'd get better. Once the doctor came and said "Now he's had a stroke, and you'll find that his brain has been affected and you really will have to have a nurse." And I said "Well let's wait until the morning anyhow until we make a decision." And in the morning when the doctor came he was sitting up reading the paper! I should think that happened about eight times.

About a fortnight before his twentieth birthday we had the awful ordeal of all the doctors involved in the case getting together and saying "Look, he'd better go to the Research Centre for cancer in London and be barrier-nursed and completely investigated because there's no reason he should be so well." It's unpleasant being investigated — it involved marrow tests which he hated — and saying "Live in this glass cubicle away from home". We were quite sure that for a home-loving boy that would be wrong.

Some months before I had had a sort of vision that he would die soon after his twentieth birthday. I had to say to the G.P. "He'll be all right till he's twenty, and that's quite soon now, and after that he'll have a few weeks' illness and he'll die. There's no point in sending him away from home before this happens." I imagine the doctors thought "Poor woman".

The day of his twentieth birthday they took a blood test and his blood count had gone right down suddenly. He had about six weeks' illness then that left him terribly bruised, and he bled from the nose for about six weeks, but he was cracking jokes, happy, a joy to be with all the way through. We nursed him ourselves, and he was having the final kind of drugs when you can't inject any more because of the bleeding — he was like a skeleton and his feet were freezing all the time. We prayed that his eyesight and his brain wouldn't be affected, and they never were. On the last afternoon he said "Would you mind staying with me as well as Pa?" So I did. I also had my little daughter to meet from school. My eldest daughter came down from London, as it were providentially, and brought her home and gave her tea. I was just able to go and say hullo, and go back, and he took my hand and said "I think I'm going". And we kissed him and said "Be with Christ."

PART THREE

Miracles

I

IN LOOKING AT the work of Burrswood we are examining one tiny corner of a matter of vast importance for humankind. For centuries we have wrestled with the problems of pain and sickness, of sin and evil, of healing and cure, seeing it now this way, now that way, in terms wholly superstitious or wholly technological, wholly irrational or wholly rational, and neither has yielded a complete answer. It seems important that we achieve some kind of synthesis between the two, recognising that both the conscious and the unconscious mind are involved in the healing process, both mind and spirit, and it is here that a place like Burrswood where religion and medicine have already worked hand in hand for many years, is already far ahead of much that is being practised elsewhere.

One of the dangers of the contemporary situation is of a polarisation into two quite different schools of healing. One is that of conventional medicine, in which treatment by drugs and surgery are commonly used. For certain kinds of illness these methods have remarkable and often quantifiable success, but in other kinds of illness (and these seem to be on the increase) they have no success at all, or the patient produces another symptom in the place of the one that has been removed. This kind of medicine has not traditionally concerned itself with the underlying states of mind which may produce illness, only with the illness itself, nor, until recently, has it asked profound questions about the extent to which a sense of meaninglessness or despair may induce illness or delay recovery. Yet even within the conventional structure there have been those who have made this correlation.

M.A.H. Melinsky quotes the superintendent of a tuberculosis sanatorium observing what first despair, and then hope, achieved for one of his patients:

> One of my most memorable patients was a young girl who hung fire for eighteen months, getting so far and no further;

> up four hours a day and walking about four hundred yards. If we tried to increase her activities, she would show unequivocal clinical deterioration and would have to be put back on absolute bed rest for a while, to start all over again. Then her jealously possessive mother, whose senile dementia had for some years been Pauline's constant anxiety, was certified as psychotic and put away in a Mental Hospital — for good. Pauline, who dearly loved her mother, shed some natural tears for a couple of days, and then started to get well; and within two months her three cavities, each larger than a walnut, which to our knowledge had been present for at least eighteen months and had been slowly worsening, completely disappeared. Six weeks later she had reached full graduated exercise and was discharged.*

Melinsky states as his opinion that such patients are suffering from 'crippling of the spirit'.

Is then 'the spirit' the answer?

If it is 'the spirit' that needs healing, if the girl was aided not by the drugs and the bed-rest of the sanatorium but by a sudden vista of renewed hope that made life livable, is then a purely spiritual approach going to be the answer to much of our suffering? At the present time there is a huge and growing interest in non-medical approaches to healing. Outside the church-setting, 'faith healers' seem to be proliferating. Within it there is a new growth of 'centres of healing', of prayer-groups for the sick, of healing services, of the practice of the laying-on of hands. This is given impetus by the 'charismatic movement', a body, mostly within the churches, which is experiencing what it believes to be an outpouring of the Holy Spirit similar to that experienced in the early church. Members find themselves 'filled with the spirit', they 'speak with tongues', they know a marvellous sense of fellowship and inspiration, and from this profound experience it seems as natural to expect healing miracles as it did for the early Christians. And already, as a result of this movement, there is a growing number of books and articles pouring from the religious presses, describing strange

*M. A. H. Melinsky, *Healing Miracles*, Mowbrays.

and apparently inexplicable events of one sort and another. These vary from artless, naïve accounts in which one feels the author might be capable of believing anything, to intellectually-disciplined accounts by very solid citizens, and what is described, in each case, is a remarkably rapid cure of disease or injury which, in the course of the body's usual healing processes, even assisted by medicine and surgery, would take weeks or months. Thus F. Roy Jeremiah describes the healing of a dog, the pet of a Vicar the author met by chance when preaching at a church in Dover.

> The dog had been ill four days, and was due for the vet if no better next day. They'd no idea as to what was wrong with it. Before leaving for church, the Vicar lifted the dog and plonked it down in a chair next to me . . . The animal flopped back and stayed put — forelegs hanging between its spread-eagled back legs, and tail dropping, altogether a picture of abject misery. Left alone, I felt rather bad eating my tea beside it . . . So I talked to it in a special tone, diffidently touching its nose with the back of my hand. It obviously had a temperature, and its eyes were very bloodshot . . . Thereupon I decided to pray for the dog. Talking quietly to it, I put my hand on its head and said a short prayer. A few minutes later I went across to the church.
>
> After service the Vicar locked up and we came through the garden in pitch darkness into a brilliantly lit kitchen. Blinking somewhat, I suddenly saw the dog rush towards me — a folded newspaper in its mouth — then it leapt right off the floor, gave a toss of the head to send a second sheet floating down; then it raced into the hall, skidding on the mats. I don't know which of us was more astonished.

Agnes Sanford, a well-known American healer, describes a train accident in which she was involved and in which a young man was injured.

> He lay drooped over the end of the seat and the blood from a gash in his forehead had already flowed in a thick stream

down the length of two train seats and was spurting very fast. Clearly I had been planted there by the Lord to be the channel of healing for this man. I leaned over the back of the seat and put my hands beneath his head, this simple human touch making a channel between person and person and between God and man. People rushed up trying to staunch the blood. The train stopped. The guard leaped to a telephone and called ahead to Havre de Grace, an unscheduled stop, for an ambulance and a doctor to meet the train. Meanwhile the flow of blood had stopped. If anyone noticed me I simply said, "I'm supporting his head." But while supporting it I continued silently to pray the prayer of faith, asking for God's healing light to come into him and to heal the wound completely and immediately. I then gave thanks that it was so . . . and I lent to the prayer the power of my imagination, seeing the wound healed. In less than ten minutes the man regained consciousness and sat up, wanting to know what all the fuss was about.

"But I don't need a doctor and an ambulance" he insisted. "I'm all right. And I don't want to go to Havre de Grace, I want to go to Philadelphia!"

However, to Havre de Grace he went, the doctor and the ambulance being already on their way. He turned as he rose to leave the train and I saw the wound on his forehead. It was only a thick white line, like a scar some three weeks old.*

Each of these stories could be paralleled in the Burrswood experience, particularly in healing incidents related to Dorothy Kerin, incidents in which bones healed, tumours disappeared, disease vanished with unaccountable speed, usually as a result of prayer or the laying-on of hands, achievements inexplicable in the light of current scientific knowledge.

It may be valuable at this stage to compare these accounts with another account of a healing, equally fast and dramatic, yet somehow not mysterious in quite the same way.

A young man was in hospital awaiting an operation for the removal of a bleeding peptic ulcer. For half an hour he

*Agnes Sanford, *The Healing Gifts of the Spirit*, Arthur James.

poured out to the chaplain a story of his own unfaithfulness to a wife who, he said, was lazy and careless. Their marriage had been a shotgun affair, and they had tried to counter its strains by having more children. The wife was worn out and unwell. Both husband and wife had themselves been illegitimate children, and had known no stability at home. Less than a week after his talk with the chaplain this patient was discharged without operation and with no visible signs of ulcer on the X-ray photograph.*

In this account there is no mention of 'prayer' or the 'laying-on of hands', only of a man pouring out the agony of his life to a sympathetic listener, and thereby apparently achieving a sort of self-healing, though this is not to minimise the skill or the faith of the supportive listener.

If it is possible to heal people so easily as the young man in the train, or even the listening chaplain, then what is our whole apparatus of hospitals, expensively-trained doctors and nurses, and costly equipment about? Prayer or a skilful listening technique will do the doctor's job for him.

There is, however, a profound difficulty about at least some of the cures that are effected by non-medical methods. It is that, since the effect of prayer, or the laying-on of hands is not quantifiable in the way that surgery or the use of drugs is quantifiable, there is really no way of measuring whether cure came by that means or by some other. In the case of the dog mentioned above, for example, what we can never know is what the dog's health would have been like if the healer had not touched him and prayed over him. Animals, like children, are sometimes capable of amazingly fast, spontaneous recovery.

To make it more complicated, there is, in many of us, a temptation to credulity that makes us delight in mysterious cures, and the belief that cure comes by way of prayer rather than by other routes. The head of a community which prays for the sick told me how on occasions, people's names have been accidentally omitted from the prayer-list, yet they or their friends have written to give thanks for an improvement in

**Healing Miracles.*

health which was seen as an answer to prayer — a prayer that was, in fact, never made.

Perhaps more disturbing than a too-glib approach to the efficacy of prayer is an excessive tendency to see Divine coincidences in all sorts of events which would strike most other observers as not particularly remarkable. The author of the book about healing in which the dog was cured saw the guiding hand of God in the fact that, at a time when he was contemplating taking up healing work in South Africa, the word South Africa seemed constantly to cross the lips of those he talked to. Yet this phenomenon is one most of us experience in mundane ways that have little to do with vocation. We have only to buy a new make of car to see cars of that make wherever we look, even if we have scarcely noticed them before.

The experience of those who pray for others is that sometimes what they have prayed for comes about and sometimes it does not. And since we can never be sure that it was not mere coincidence that what was prayed for came about, it is easy to feel discouraged, sceptical, and willing only to give consent to the kind of healing that is quantifiable and which needs no extraordinary faith. Yet then the danger comes of throwing the baby out with the bathwater, because 'Divine healing' of the kind practised at Burrswood or at Lourdes does have remarkable successes that are not due to medical intervention and which are generally accredited as such. We cannot get away with dismissing 'miracle', as I tried to do when I first went to Burrswood. Whether we like it or not (and I didn't like it) it is something which happens, and which has to be taken up into our understanding of healing and our treatment of sickness.

What, we should ask at this point, is a miracle? Evelyn Frost, in her book *Christian Healing*, defines it as 'a wonderful phenomenon usually associated with some event in which the law of causation cannot be observed.'* She does not see God as disturbing the coherence and unity of his creation by breaking his own physical laws, but feels rather that miracle comes within the field of the 'unrationalized as yet'. She points out that many phenomena which were once classified as miraculous are so no

*Evelyn Frost, *Christian Healing,* Mowbrays.

longer — for example, eclipses, thunderstorms, earthquakes, volcanic eruptions, are now recognised as phenomena which conform to natural laws which are known to us, though they once seemed inexplicable except in terms of God's direct intervention. In the light of a deeper knowledge man had to sacrifice some of his credulity.

There is much that man does not know, vast areas of knowledge that are so far entirely beyond his ken, but in the light of new discoveries he will be obliged to revise his thinking, as the theory of relativity obliged him to revise his theory of gravity and the discovery of the electron changed his understanding of the structure and behaviour of matter. At the present stage of our understanding many cures are effected, by way of prayer, or the laying-on of hands, that we can only call 'miracle' because they do not 'fit in' with our understanding of natural laws in the way that the use of chemicals does. This is not to say that they will always appear as miracles; some, like the story of the chaplain and the man with the peptic ulcer, may have a psychological explanation; some may conform to a telepathic law of which modern civilised man is ignorant, though his ancestors may well have known something of it; some, particularly those connected with touching, may be making use of some force akin to electricity which is felt but not seen. The more we know about such laws the more accurately and precisely we can help one another, and for those who love their fellow men enough to want to help them there is the paradox that instead of giving 'God' or 'Christ' or 'the Holy Spirit' as the immediate and only source of the event, as is usually the case with miracle, we may help more if we laboriously attempt to chart some of the unknown territory in between the Divine source, God and the healing event. It is as Divine intervention retreats that man begins to gain some understanding and control over the world around him. Primitive man sees everything as directly controlled and supervised by God or the gods — the rain, the thunder, the famine, the epidemic — and he is wracked alternately by wonder and fear. More civilised man experiences God more distantly — he is aware of laws or agencies which cause such events to happen and is not so inclined to see in them expressions of God's anger or disapproval. He does not believe that the thunder indicates Divine rage, or that cerebral haemorrhage is a 'stroke' sent as a deliberate punishment by God. This makes his world perhaps duller, but less fearful.

It need not, in my view, mean that God is ignored, but that rather we have to stretch our minds to a new and more complex understanding of him. In 'Diving healing' circles there is perhaps a tendency to talk rather cosily of 'God' or 'Christ' or 'the Holy Spirit' as a kind of co-partner in the healing enterprise when, as in the case of the chaplain, the immediate explanation is more mundane. What really matters, perhaps, is that the whole enterprise of healing, of whatever kind, should be seen as part of Divine purpose, with Christ present as much in the attentive chaplain or the nurse as in a priest giving the laying-on of hands or kneeling in prayer.

If we place the whole enterprise of healing within the context of the divine purpose, with the kinds of healing of which we know the rational explanation given their rightful place, and with prayer employed as a way of moving forward in the darkness towards the kinds of healing we know we need but as yet do not know how to achieve, then we have a chance to chart some of that unknown territory between the two which at present is simply known by the name of 'miracle'. 'Miracle' becomes the all-embracing name for a mixed bag of phenomena which at the moment we can only ascribe to God's direct intervention, but which in time we may learn to ascribe to physical or psychological causes. What we cannot know is whether there is a hard core of events that are 'purely' spiritual, that will always defy explanations, because in them God is, in fact, defying his own laws. Some of us will want to come down on one side of this argument and some on the other, according to our beliefs about the kind of God who deals with us. But whichever side we choose, it is wise to respect 'miracle' as a 'way in' to new understanding, and to be grateful for what it achieves.

If we start from a basis of Christian belief it is not really possible to ignore that a sense of a healing mission was central to Christ's understanding of himself and of the work that his disciples were to perform. His function was principally a reconciling and liberating one, reconciling mankind with God, liberating men from their sins, setting them free into a more abundant life where they were not hampered by fear. He regarded certain sorts of behaviour which societies often think of as sinful, e.g. prostitution, as more in the nature of a sickness, whereas excessive moral righteousness accompanied by censoriousness he seemed to regard as a dangerous and wicked personal state. Confronted by sickness, in some forms though by no means in all, he gave an act of absolution which suggests that he thought that sin, and the guilt consequent upon it, played a key role in the illness. For example, in the case of the man with the palsy whose friends let him down on a stretcher from the roof-top, he used the words "Son, thy sins be forgiven thee". Was this, we may wonder, a reference to actual deeds committed by this paralysed man, or a recognition that his paralysis was an irreligious retreat from the real demands of living, and that breaking out of his fear itself constituted a return to God that absolved him of sin?

Although some scholars, such as Bultmann, have tried to deny that miracles played an important part in the life of Christ and the founding of the Church, or that they actually occurred at all, it needs an extraordinary distortion of the mood of the Gospels either to say that they didn't happen or that they can be easily explained away in terms of suggestion and the overcoming of conversion hysteria. Such incidents as the healing of the man with the withered hand show that even Jesus' enemies took it for granted that he *could* heal sickness; their only uncertainty was whether he would do so on the Sabbath.

Again the way the healing of sickness was taken for granted as an important function of the Early Church, and the way Christianity for many years was the most important focus of healing activity in Europe, laying the basis for modern medicine, suggests that there was a time when the remarkable became, for a period, unremarkable, just as the healing power of Jesus became unremarkable to the Pharisees. Miracles happened so often that they became, temporarily, part of the normal course of experience.

Many who witnessed the way Christians endured under the persecution of Nero felt that they were seeing a particular sort of miracle; they certainly saw human beings suffering and dying in a manner unfamiliar to them. Cyprian writes of this extraordinary sight:-

> I, indeed, have known it . . . when the cruel hands of the persecutors were wrenching asunder the martyr's limbs, and the furious torturer was ploughing up his lacerated muscles, and still could not overcome him . . . I have known it by the words of those who stood around. This is a great matter. Assuredly I know not what it is — that he is not subdued by suffering, that he is not broken down by wearing torments . . . This matter must be known, and this strength must be investigated, even to the very heart; for that is no trifling confession, whatever it may be, for which a man suffers, even so as to be able to die.

Similar events have occasionally been noted in our own time, as in the case of Mother Maria Skobstova described by Sergei Hackel in *A Pearl of Great Price* who was similarly calm and serene under the blows, abuse and deprivation of Ravensbruck concentration camp. Are we dealing with a case of dissociation, a mental blocking by the person of the reality of suffering, a kind of self-brain-washing, (or in the case of the Early Christians a collective brain-washing) or are we looking at something more unusual? Possibly at the ability of some individuals or groups who have undergone exceptional experiences of love and healing, to perceive the brain-washing inherent in our usual understanding of 'reality', particularly in regard to suffering, and thus to break through to a new position in which the suffering is not simply destructive but is perceived as creative?

There are records of Christ's disciples, after his death, healing the sick, casting out demons, raising the dead. It took the experience of the Resurrection to enable them to do this, since while Christ was still alive they could only heal fitfully, and sometimes not at all. Their experience of life was still somehow incomplete; they lacked some maturity, some healing within their own personalities which would make them free enough to liberate others.

Yet are all healers liberated people? Tacitus gives an amusing story of the Roman Emperor Vespasian being forced into a position where he had to attempt to cure two suppliants.

> One of the common folk of Alexandria, known for his blindness, flung himself down before his (Vespasian's) knees, begging and sighing for a cure for his blindness, on the advice of the god Serapis . . . and he begged the emperor to deign to moisten his cheeks and his eye-sockets with his spittle; another, with a sick hand, begged the emperor, on the advice of the same god, to tread on him with his foot. At first Vespasian turned away, laughing, but when they persisted he now feared the rumour that a failure would cause, and then was encouraged by their pleas and the voices of the coaxers; finally he commanded that physicians should examine whether such blindness and impotence could be cured by human effort. After lengthy consultations the physicians judged that the power of sight of the one had not been destroyed and would return when the impediments were dislodged, and that the crooked limbs of the other could be restored if beneficial power were applied; this was perhaps after the heart of the gods, and the emperor had been chosen as the divine instrument; finally, if the cure were successful the fame thereof would accrue to the emperor, whereas if it failed, scorn would be the lot of the unfortunate couple. And so Vespasian, with a glad countenance, and believing that all was open to his fortune and nothing more was unbelievable, complied with the urgent prayers, which the crowd standing by watched with rapt attention: at once the hand could be used again and the daylight shone again for the blind man.

Psychologically, this is a fascinating story. The two sick men approached Vespasian, not because of his wholeness, or because of his reputation as a healer, but because they are awed by the *mana* of his office. Their belief in his power is such that they cannot believe that even sickness could withstand it, and their belief is all the greater because they are simple men, not troubled by intellectual theories and scepticism. There is nothing 'clever' about their approach. Vespasian's own attitude is almost equally interesting. By the time he has finished talking to his advisers, he half believes in his own power to heal, and embarks upon the experiment with excitement and interest. Like other monarchs, holy men, and even doctors one can think of, he half believes the myth that surrounds him, and this gives him the strength to do something for which, at first, he doubts his own capacity. Somewhere within this story — in the minds, it would seem of the suppliants rather than in the power of the healer — are the ingredients needed for the kind of rapid healing called a miracle — power and meaning, even if, as in this case, it is worldly power and meaning, and absolute faith of a sort that perhaps few people actually possess. It is possible to imagine some moderns being cured by a similar faith in the Royal Family, and of course, the sight or touch of a monarch was long thought to be healing. (Dr. Johnson, as a child, was brought to see Queen Anne passing in procession, in the hope of curing his scrofula). But then emperors and monarchs were often thought to be of Divine origin, or at least to occupy the throne by 'Divine right' so that they were part of the chain of meaning, and so of healing, that passed from God to man. The two sick men are responding not to a rather foolish and worldly man, but to the near-holiness with which they regard his office, an office which for them seems to open a window upon divinity.

The difference between Christ and Vespasian was that Christ did, in fact, incarnate the divinity in which his patients believed, whereas Vespasian did so only by virtue of his office, yet the awe associated with office clearly plays an important part in healing, whether in the temple healings of Aesculapius, the spiritual counselling of priests in the Christian tradition, or the particular kind of awe with which consultants are treated in a modern hospital setting. What surrounds each is a reputation for healing power.

In the early days of Christianity the disciples of Christ had a reputation for healing power, partly because of the power derived from having known and lived with Jesus, partly because a sense of power continued to flow through them, to be part of their daily experience, and this power flowed outwards, curing the possessed, the deformed, the disabled and the diseased. No doubt this posed for them a real problem of 'inflation' as it did for Dorothy Kerin — it is not easy to continue to see oneself as an 'ordinary person' when one daily performs extraordinary deeds — and it is a tribute to their psychological balance, as it was to hers, that they never ceased to preserve a humble attitude to their gift, seeing themselves as instruments and agents and not as prime movers in the healing process. Something is moving through them that works creatively in the world; they do not know, nor do they need to know, precisely what it is or how it works, but they know where, or who, it comes from. They are the focus.

In addition to power, such healers often exhibit a striking sense of harmony with the world about them, harmony with the other creatures who make up that world. The Alexandrian Fathers of the fourth century, quite a long way away in time from the great outpouring of the Spirit in the Early Church, have a reputation for having lived on good terms with the wild beasts of the desert, unafraid of them and unmolested by them, almost as if they were inhabiting an unfallen world, Eden before the Fall. Like Christ and his disciples they exhibited great shrewdness and insight in dealing with men. Perhaps because of the self-knowledge that was painfully but unavoidably acquired in the conditions of the desert they perceived underlying motives of which those who consulted them were often unaware themselves, and so uncovered the distortions of neuroticism which often lead men and women to withdraw from life into sickness. And they had, of course, a powerful sense of evil, which torments the solitary, and pursues the worldly, pushing men into wrong choices and bad solutions.

The power, harmony, perception and knowledge of sin that marked the Christian gift of healing were to continue right through Christian history, but sadly, they were to become so special and unusual that only the occasional holy man or woman, the 'saint' (using the term in a different way from the way the Early Christians had used it as a kind of commonplace of their religious experience) was still able to heal in the striking and dramatic way that Christ and his disciples had done. (It would be wrong, however, to underestimate the healing power of many lesser men and women — the sort who, by being loving parents, or friends, or pastors, or good teachers or employers or artists, have always had a creative effect on those around them.) St. Francis, St. Teresa. St. John of the Cross, St. Catherine of Genoa and many, many more, all achieved healing miracles.

In 1858 Bernadette Soubirous, an uneducated adolescent girl from a poverty-stricken family in the French Pyrenees, had a vision of the Immaculate Conception at Massabielle, near Lourdes, and within a few years Lourdes became a centre of healing which is an extraordinary success in drawing crowds to the present day. A million pilgrims a year visit the shrine, coming from all over the world to drink or bathe in the waters of the fountain, to kiss the rock where the Virgin appeared, and to pray at the shrine. The Virgin instructed Bernadette to pray and do penance for the sin and suffering of the world, and to build a church for her there. Within a short time the first healing miracle took place, and since then many others have claimed miracles. These are all very carefully examined, and only those where there are existing medical reports which show the patient's condition before visiting Lourdes to have been radically different are accepted. The 'proved' miracles come to 54 in all, according to Melinsky, not very many in view of the vast numbers who go to the shrine, yet nevertheless of crucial importance to those who were involved. Melinsky points out that the Roman Catholic authorities sternly disallow any illness which may have a psychosomatic origin, yet he feels they do not take sufficient account of the emotional factors which may play a part in illnesses such as cancer and tuberculosis, and both these diseases figure largely in the list of miraculous cures.

Those who visit Lourdes and see the long lines of desperately sick people praying together and receiving blessing, or the parents wheeling terribly deformed and diseased children through the streets, may feel that Lourdes' major miracle is of a different order; it is to bring hope, joy, faith into lives which have been deeply stricken by suffering.

The vision of Bernadette, and the miracles which follow it, have the same characteristics of power, harmony, insight and awareness of sin that we noted in the earlier Christian miracles, but it is striking that the power had, in this instance, notably feminine characteristics, both in the person of the Virgin, and in the symbolism; the cave, the fountain, the roses (all feminine symbols) all played an important part in the event. A Jungian interpretation of Bernadette's vision would suggest that unconsciously she was correcting the masculine bias of the Church, revealing, with a knowledge that went far beyond her conscious intelligence or understanding, that femininity, particularly in a maternal form, was needed, both collectively and individually, for healing, and this interpretation is borne out by the similar revelation to the Pope, only a few years before, of the Immaculate Conception. Manifestations of this kind were 'in the air' as it were. Devotion to Mary as mother still plays a very important part in the prayers of Lourdes — public prayers made in the square before the Basilica refer to the whole gathering, not just the obviously stricken, as sick children turning to Mary for comfort and help.

Some of that remarkable power that manifested itself at Lourdes, has also manifested itself at Burrswood; clothed in different forms, since the time and place were different, yet once again exhibiting the special qualities of power, harmony with creation, insight and awareness of sin. People came, and come, to Burrswood in need of a tender understanding of their sufferings, of love, of renewed hope. Some come to die, and others to begin life all over again. Some, only a few, as at Lourdes, experience miracle in the sense of a rapid and scientifically inexplicable healing. Some undergo a miraculous change in their emotions. Some gain the courage to face intolerable facts. Some take a long look at wrongdoing, either in the sense of destructive deeds, or in the attempt to escape from the demands of life, trying to live without living, bound by neurotic fears.

Dorothy Kerin, who set this work in motion, has something of the same simplicity as Bernadette, the sense that she was taken up and used, and that it was the purpose that was important and not she herself.

2

Sickness

SICKNESS AND PAIN are so much part of our world that it is difficult for us to stand far enough back from them to see them with any sort of clarity. From infancy, even the healthiest of us suffer minor pains and illnesses — the pain of cutting teeth, the pain of falling and hurting ourselves, the pain of epidemic illnesses accompanied by fever, sore throats, rashes and coughs. We know about physical wretchedness and early in our lives make a commonsense resolution to avoid it if we possibly can. On the other hand we may simultaneously learn that illness has certain gains — that it secures for us the attention, interest and loving care of others, which sets up a certain ambiguity in our attitude to illness. We don't want pain and discomfort, but there are occasions when it may be better than the alternative — the sense of being ignored, unwanted and unloved.

Illness can have other gains too. It can help us to escape temporarily from some of the strains of living — in the case of the child, from the strains of school. It can keep us, for as long as it lasts, in a safe, comfortable environment (home), where we don't have to compete or struggle. It returns us to the blissful dependence and irresponsibility of infancy.

I suppose there are few of us who have not, in childhood, played upon illness to get attention or to escape from school, and we remember the sense of mingled shame and satisfaction it aroused in us; some of us, even in our adult illnesses, can detect a longing to be let off the full rigour of living for a while. Some, the hysterics, can dodge life altogether by this route, tragically depriving themselves of the real gains of adventure, work, love and life for the pitiful substitute of invalidism. Yet even these, as we see in the case of Elizabeth Barrett Browning, can be lured back to life on occasions, if the incentive is strong enough to encourage them to break out of their prison.

For most of us, however, illness has more complex roots. We may be born of a family that shows a particular tendency to succumb to a particular disease; we may be the victim of accident, or of circumstances, such as poor living conditions or overwork which predispose us to illness; we may have a sudden shock, such as a bereavement, which seems to initiate a physical illness; we may have bad habits, such as over-eating, or drinking, or smoking too much, which tend to bring about physical damage. We may dimly see that our asthma, or our ulcers, or our arthritis or our colitis, is not an accidental happening, but is associated with our fear, our longing for dependence, our anger, our anxiety, or our struggle to make good in a competitive world. This does not in itself necessarily help, since we may have little idea how to deal with these destructive emotions; it only takes us one step back towards the roots of our illness.

Perhaps this is better, however, than much traditional medicine that has not encouraged patients to take any responsibility at all for their own illness. According to this school of thought, now dying rapidly, at least among younger doctors, the patient was little more than a body to be treated chemically or surgically, and possibly to be given an occasional patronising pep-talk since morale (interpreted as blind faith in the skill of the doctor) was also acknowledged to have a place in healing. In this kind of treatment the patient was thrust firmly into an inferior position — like a child or a subordinate he was expected to do what he was told without even having the treatment explained to him. He was not a partner in the enterprise, nor encouraged to co-operate for his own good.

As a young woman expecting my first baby I paid a routine visit to a famous maternity hospital. The consultant entered my cubicle and without a word to me, not even "Good afternoon", began a series of very painful manipulations of my body, the purpose of which I had not the faintest idea. My attempts to ask and protest were met only by the sharp response "Be quiet". He left me, again without a word, shaking, terrified, and in tears, and when I asked the sister what had happened, she explained that the baby was in the wrong position for birth and that he had turned it, successfully. I was grateful for what was achieved, but to this day remain puzzled that my co-operation, in relaxing and generally not resisting, was not invited, and even more puzzled that a man whose life's work was the welfare of women and babies, was content to adopt such a brutal and humiliating social technique. It was *my* baby and *my* body, and the brutal invasion of its privacy without explanation or consent was a kind of rudimentary rape.

Yet whatever the failures of *that* school of medicine, it did work after a fashion. The consultant *did* turn my baby so that she had a normal birth, much surgery and medicine did and does remove disease and relieve pain, sending people back from hospital to lead normal working and family lives. However much we may criticise conventional medicine, its achievements, particularly in the last half century, have been astonishing, with tuberculosis, smallpox, diphtheria, poliomyelitis almost totally controlled in this country and others, and other illnesses, such as heart disease, kidney disease, and some forms of cancer, substantially helped by mechanical devices, surgery and drugs. Some doctors have begun to suggest that we may be coming to the end of that great period of advance — that what *can* be cured by existing methods has been, and we are gradually coming up against illnesses that will prove intractable to such means — but even if this is so, the wonderful relief and liberation from suffering that has been realised, in itself a kind of miracle, must always be a cause for gratitude and hope.

That kind of medicine worked, and in a modified form continues to work, because it had real power. There was the *mana* of the doctor, perhaps heightened, particularly among ignorant people, by his rather lordly attitude, and there was skill and devotion. Insight into the patient's emotional or other problems was not usually thought to be necessary, at least in a hospital setting (the old-fashioned G.P. often knew a great deal about his patients and their lives). Psychology was not part of the doctor's training.

Perhaps this kind of healing is so successful, even though it short-circuits emotional problems, just because in most patients the will to recover is so strong. Many people may need a temporary reprieve from living, but most would rather live than not live, so that the patient co-operates with the doctor even without an invitation to do so, just by his determination to get well. But the following example, quoted by Melinsky, shows how helpless conventional medicine can be, where the patient does *not* wish to recover.

'A young woman suddenly lost a father and, soon after, a sister of whom she was very fond. She was left at the mercy of a possessive mother and dominating aunt. She developed ulcerative colitis, together with a deep depression, and was operated on for the removal of part of the colon. The operation was successful, but she died a few days later.'*

Such patients suffered from a system of healing that did not take account of the whole person, but insisted on treating the sick only as a body. And it follows naturally that where the patient is treated only as a body the method of care becomes impersonal, without great regard for the emotional needs of the patient, a danger heightened by the immense pressure and the shortage of money under which our hospital system has long had to work. Since the society in which the patients become ill also shows signs of depersonalisation, and since it is at least arguable that there is a correlation between this depersonalisation and some of the illnesses from which patients suffer, it is possible that the healing methods often employed may exacerbate rather than help the condition of sickness. The kind of patient whose illness is a 'cry for help' may not necessarily find it in a treatment which cares nothing about the conditions of his life, a treatment which is, in fact, simply the stifling of the cry.

Is this unfair to the modern hospital? Dr. Michael Wilson, writing out of hospital experience both in England and abroad, remarks that the doctor is a 'technical expert', whose function is 'cure' rather than 'care'. He feels that it is a comment on our attitude that the nurse's skill, which is 'care' rather than 'cure' is less valued and less well paid than that of the doctor. 'Cure' seems to carry a less personal approach; he quotes a surgeon's remark 'We can cure people these days without even

***Healing Miracles*.

knowing their names.' This emphasis on cure at the expense of care means that caring for its own sake no longer seems so important, and those patients who show little hope of 'cure' — the mentally subnormal, the geriatric, and some psychiatric cases — have fewer resources spent on them, and attract fewer recruits to work amongst them. There is no 'glamour' attached to such work, since our society does not value it.

Within a society which sets cure above care, the role of the nurse also begins to change.

> If there is a high expectation among patients and their families that disease will be cured, and this is what society values, then the nursing profession may attract nurses who find fulfilment in more medical and technical kinds of work. In fact most student nurses at present seem to come for training with a desire to care for people: but the system of training tends to crush it out of them. There is not necessarily a contradiction between curing disease and caring for patients, but an unbalanced training in clinical objectivity, and the discouragement of personal relationships between nurse and patient may result in a more impersonal style of nursing.*

Another problem Dr. Wilson sees about the hospital is the dependence it forces upon patients.

> The very word patient — the one who suffers — denotes one who is passive, who submits to the authority of skilled professionals who know what is best for him. Staff adopt a "We'll take care of you" attitude which gives the patient and his relatives confidence. Not only then do patients regress as a part of the withdrawal from active life imposed by or expressed in illness, but the whole milieu of hospital life also favours regression. The patient is put to bed (sometimes unnecessarily), and deprived of his clothes. Encouraged by the strong attitudes of staff, he is reduced to dependence and compliance . . . Few patients need to be treated as passive all the time. Most patients are responsible agents to some extent,

*Michael Wilson, *Health is for People,* DLT.

even if only ten per cent responsible. Many are ninety per cent or more capable of making choices and entering into partnership with staff in the work of making a good recovery. In conditions like alcoholism the acceptance of full responsibility by the person himself or herself may be the key to progress.

The refusal of hospital staff to give information to the patient rather than his relatives, and in some cases the refusal even to take relatives into their confidence, are also seen by Dr. Wilson as part of the present failure.

His basic objection to the system is the underlying assumption that every problem has a solution, and that death is the worst thing that can happen to a human being, two ideas new to the thought of our society which seem to have a stultifying and degrading effect on our values.

In the West we try to reach health by the eradication of such defects as can be cured, by the solution of such problems as may be solved, and by a denial of the incurable and the insoluble by their exclusion into institutions . . . Death, the great insoluble incurable fact, is denied. This denial of death is the root cause of our denials of its foreshadowings. Death is believed to be dominant over life. We really do believe in death: talk of resurrection and the future life is thought to be fantasy. Sartre vividly describes in his novels the resultant meaninglessness which has spread through life. Medicine cannot but share in this loss of meaning, for the style of being a doctor is influenced by the society and culture of the day.

If we are unhappy with the hospital and the medical centre, what other methods are there for treatment? Doctors are rightly suspicious of quackery, sensing that the power and the financial rewards available to those who are able, or who pretend to be able, to cure, are a temptation to the unscrupulous, and in their effort to save the public from such villains they go to great lengths to insist on proper apprenticeship and the exclusion of the untrained from the ranks of healers.

There is an obvious wisdom in this, yet also certain serious drawbacks. One is that healing is turned into an esoteric art, beyond the understanding of all who have not been drilled in current methods, and the concern with the issues of sickness and health which necessarily affects everyone born into this world is lifted beyond the reach of the ordinary person into the field of the 'expert'. Of course, many of the refinements of modern medicine are beyond the understanding of the layman, yet we may feel that a basic understanding of, and education in, the workings of mind and body, are everyone's birthright, and are a necessity if we are to co-operate with healers in keeping ourselves healthy, or correct our way of life if we are sick. The man or woman who has been implicitly trained to believe that such matters do not concern him or her becomes the sucker who is constantly pleading for more drug prescriptions, or who indulges persistently in habits of living liable to bring about an early death or at least a serious physical breakdown.

Yet many elements in our society are now working to undermine this old authoritarian view of medicine. One of them, as one of the doctors who works at Burrswood pointed out to me, is the great interest the mass media, and television in particular, take in medical science. Working as a G.P. he finds his patients primed in new techniques of which he has not always yet learned himself. This is not always a good thing, yet he feels it tears away some of the veils with which, often unnecessarily, medicine has been clothed, and encourages people to think more intelligently, and often more sympathetically, about physical and mental illness.

Another element at work in changing attitudes to conventional medicine is the way that in more primitive societies, where there are simply not enough doctors to do all the work that needs to be done, others are trained to perform basic medical tasks which, in this country, only a doctor would perform. It is not perhaps very desirable that this should be emulated here unless some emergency forces it upon us, but it does suggest that the gap between doctor and layman is not as huge and insurmountable as we have sometimes believed, and that some of the simpler tasks might be performed by laymen under supervision, as in fact they are by medical students in training.

Much more important than either of these is the fact that many, many men and women have natural gifts of healing, gifts that are largely squandered in our present society. These may take the form of an exceptionally cheerful and positive personality, the sort that makes the hopeless and the depressed feel better just by appearing. Or they may take the form of a natural capacity for listening, or for physically caring for people who are ill or disabled. Others seem to have gifts that we know less about, a touch that seems to have healing properties, or, much more mysteriously, a diagnostic gift. An American neuro-psychiatrist, Dr. Shafica Karagulla, made careful tests of a large number of people with extra-sensory gifts.* Between them they could do all kinds of apparently inexplicable things from water-divining to psychometry (knowing about the associations of a particular object without knowing the owner) but the most remarkable of all was a woman called Diane, who had no medical training. Diane could diagnose almost any condition of sickness — a growth in the colon so far undetected, heart disease, epilepsy (and even the fact that the patient had previously had part of the brain removed by surgery) and often the emotional condition of the patient, just by sitting opposite the person and looking. She claimed to do it by seeing — what she saw when she looked at the patient was an energy force field which existed in and around the patient and within which she could perceive their organs responding either healthily or unhealthily. Not only could she detect current illness with perfect accuracy (allowing for a certain naïvety of description because of her lack of formal training), but she could also tell when something was *beginning* to go wrong with a patient, so that they were liable to become ill within six months or so.

We may feel that such gifts as Diane's are so unusual as to be scarcely worth taking into general consideration, yet Dr. Karagulla's researches revealed an extraordinary number of 'sensitives', none of them with quite Diane's gift, but each with some unexpected and frequently useful gift of their own. There were a number with a 'healing touch', including one man who

*Shafica Karagulla, *Breakthrough to Creativity,* De Vorss & Co. Inc.

was particularly successful with headaches and stomach aches, there were those who could identify with another's body to the point of feeling pain where they felt it, and there were many who had diagnostic gifts of one kind and another. Amongst those with healing and diagnostic gifts were a great many doctors, who had long made use of their extra-sensory gifts to help their patients, while usually concealing their strange abilities from everyone because they did not 'fit in' with the scientific ethos in which they had been brought up. In each case they had feared themselves abnormal in their uniqueness, and had been afraid that others would think them crazy or professionally unsound if they told the truth about their methods. One doctor had a precognitive gift which told him with unerring accuracy whether or not a patient would recover from an operation and he always turned out to be right even when colleagues thought he had made the wrong decision. Another knew when patients in whom he had a particular interest had taken a turn for the worse and needed his attention. One woman doctor could sense movements of circulation and of brain fluids by touching her patients, and make useful deductions from what she felt. A consultant at the Mayo Clinic could 'see' any organ in his patient's body and knew what was wrong with them within a few moments of their arriving in his office, though he always went through the routine laboratory tests to avoid arousing comment. Several of such people mentioned that others in their family had similar gifts.

Dr. Karagulla did not find these gifts particularly bizarre, but felt that they conformed to a pattern often noted in geniuses of one kind or another to arrive at a result that would not only be beyond the achievement of most ordinary people, but which does not always seem to bear much relation to the knowledge, or intellectual and sensory equipment of the person concerned, the 'intuitive effect' often mentioned by scientists, inventors, artists and others who often themselves cannot explain how they arrived at their particular answer, solution, discovery or inspiration. She feels that the healing gifts described are no different in kind from the (well-attested) gifts of a recent Professor in Mathematics at Edinburgh, Professor Aitken. This mathematical genius could sit down and write out a whole symphony from memory when he had seen the score only once. He could scan a book briefly and then dictate the whole contents from memory. He could answer the most complicated mathematical problems more quickly than the electronic computer, recall over a thousand numbers read out to him in order, either backwards or forwards, and perform many more unusual feats of this kind. Two of his brothers had similar gifts. Dr. Karagulla speculates that such abilities may be associated with man's evolutionary attempt to improve his adaptation to the environment; that such individuals, developing parts of the human brain which have so far lain dormant, may be the next step in mankind's struggle towards growth.

The gifts she examined concerned many other fields besides healing, but so far as healing is concerned her work started two interesting trains of thought. One is that many practising doctors are possessed of special healing gifts that go beyond conventional training, or a pleasant 'bedside manner', although our present understanding of what is 'proper' in a doctor, and what a rigorous scientific manner consists of, makes it necessary for them to conceal the form their genius takes. It might be valuable if a medical body undertook a confidential survey to see how many doctors feel themselves to be gifted in this way. The other is that many people who may have neither the intelligence, the education, nor the inclination to become doctors or nurses might have healing abilities they could contribute to the general good, either in a diagnostic capacity (one which obviously would need careful supervision) or in the matter of 'the healing touch'.

Dr. Karagulla's 'sensitives' with their remarkable ability to 'see' what is wrong with sick people, do not regard themselves as caught up in an esoteric, mystical or 'spiritual' experience. They are not necessarily people of any religious belief, and their gift is to them perfectly ordinary though they have learned, sometimes painfully, that the world may think them barmy or freakish. What a number of them describe is a different perception of the human body from that common among the rest of us.

One of the things that intrigued me most and was most baffling as I talked . . . was their mention of an energy field around the body and interpenetrating the body. Some of them saw this energy field in much more detail than others did. They were able to note variations in the field which assisted them in diagnosis. There were a few who saw vortices of energy at certain points along the spine, connected with or influencing the endocrine system. This energy field they described as a living, moving web of frequency intimately connected with conditions in the physical body . . . As I continued to work with Diane she was able to repeatedly predict the onset of a disease or to indicate the progress of a disease by what she saw in the energy body or web . . . The total structure of this energy body which Diane and other individuals sees shows the same kind of variation as different types of physical bodies in different individuals. For example, the whole web of energy may appear to her as tightly woven or loosely woven, as coarse or fine, as dull or bright. It may extend as much as two inches beyond the physical body or less than an inch. In conditions of disease it may show a wide range of disturbances. There may be loss in the energy field, breaks in the pattern, tiny whirlpools of energy that have broken off from the normal stream, gaps in the web, or a jumble of lines of force like scar tissue. All of these things Diane relates to conditions in the physical body in consistent and accurate observation.

Other 'sensitives' who also had 'the healing touch' also had different experiences. One doctor said that she could feel energy passing from her hands to the patient, another that patients often felt heat from his touch, and a third that he was aware himself of nothing unusual happening but that pain stopped when he touched an afflicted part.

It is interesting to compare these reports with the accounts of miracle and laying-on of hands given elsewhere in this book, and it is obvious that there is an overlap of experience. The special insight of the healer, whether religious or not, includes particular perceptions of a patient's physical and emotional condition which would be beyond most observers, and of which the healer himself may be only half-consciously aware. Similarly the 'healing touch' may be administered either within the simple but careful ritual of the healing service or in the home or hospital setting. How important then *is* the religious setting or the acknowledgement of a religious dimension? Is prayer a necessary part of the process at all?

To a Christian healer like the American Agnes Sanford, prayer is central to the healing experience — 'Healing is only answered prayer' she quotes a friend as saying, 'And anyone can learn to pray'. Prayer then is a method not for the unusually gifted, but simply for those who care about their fellow men and long to help.

Agnes Sanford describes herself, in middle age, passing into a depressive breakdown, gradually emerging by means of her own prayers and those of others, longing to pass on the gift of healing she has received, praying for such a gift, and then discovering that it has, in fact, been given to her. This is the beginning of an unusual ministry of speaking and writing, and above all of receiving an unending stream of visitors with physical or mental troubles to whom she gives the laying-on of hands. Mrs. Sanford believes in a literal interpretation of biblical promises, which at times is not all that far from fundamentalism, and she has little interest in seeking alternative language for the events she describes, in trying to look at them, for example, from a psychological point of view. Yet despite the slightly rigid Christian approach, there is a real wisdom, shrewdness, and love, in her approach to despair, sickness and health, and her shining belief in the efficacy of prayer is impressive. She has the Puritan understanding of the damage wrought in the personality by guilt, of the need for self-knowledge, and of the importance of acting on our insights, limited as these may be. She is fully aware of how dangerous the sense of power associated with healing can become, sees the need for the healer constantly to recognise his own sickness and frailty, is wary of too glib a belief in 'possession' and feels that in any case no one should ever be told they are 'possessed', though if they claim that this is their trouble their belief should be taken seriously. Above all, her understanding of the Christian healing role is that 'the gifts of the Spirit' are available to mankind exactly as they were in the first century, and believers have only to pray for the gifts and open themselves to the experience, to be able to heal as their forebears did. It is significant that she does not see the healing act as an individual enterprise — the individual healer acts always on behalf of the Christian community, sustained at every point by their prayers and fellowship and interest, an approach squarely within the Apostolic tradition. Within that tradition she suggests what she feels is the correct approach to healing. She is writing of the individual praying about his own suffering, but she goes on to suggest that the same technique should be applied to praying for others:

> (a) Choose which symptom or weakness you will pray about first and do not try to pray for all of them at once.
>
> (b) Form your prayer in words that suggest to the body the healed condition and not the continuing trouble. For every cell in the body has a rudimentary reaction and will respond to your words. For instance, I learned in praying for the healing of migraine headaches not to pray "Please don't let me have headaches any more" for the very word 'headache' suggested headaches to the body-mind . . . I worked out this form of prayer: "Come into me, O Lord, and heal the blood of the body so that it flows from head to foot in perfect order and harmony with no congestion anywhere." The headaches were not completely healed until years later when the memories were healed, but they became much better from the time that I began to pray this prayer once a day.
>
> (c) Make, in the imagination, a picture of the thing that you desire in prayer. Hold this picture in the mind as much as possible, but lightly, as one plays a game. When, for a time, symptoms recur, bring the picture back to mind and speak consolingly to the body, saying in effect, "Never mind, here is the picture of what shall be and we are on our way

to it." Do not scold the body. Understand that a healing of trouble such as this, brought on by the pressures of life, requires time. There is nothing to be frightened about if it does not take place at once.

(d) Give thanks to God that His Power is entering and is working toward wholeness in the body in all ways best according to His will.

Yes, you give thanks before you see the healing . . . You say "Thank you" when a friend offers to do a favour for you. It is the natural and courteous thing, and it keeps the way open so that the favour can be done . . . All prayer is in essence an attempt to work out and establish what we believe to be God's will. When we go to a doctor (which we are free to do, because prayer does not rule out medical care any more than it rules out the eating of food), we take for granted that it is right to seek healing — in other words that it is according to the will of God.*

For Agnes Sanford the prayer of healing is partly a matter of making positive suggestions to the body, partly an imaginative exercise into what it would be like to be whole, partly a movement of gratitude for a world which works towards wholeness and healing. It is not difficult to imagine that many could be helped by such an approach.

Nevertheless, there does seem to be a difficulty about such a method that is not always fully faced by Christians. The emphasis in such a healing approach is always on asking 'in perfect faith' with the implication that if the faith is perfect then the healing will come. Yet for many with long-standing disabilities which may have involved very costly and painful adjustments — blindness, say, or paraplegia — perfect faith in cure may be too risky an emotional experience to undertake. To pray as if it had already happened, and to give thanks for it, when the medical prognosis is poor and when other attempts at cure have failed, may conjure up a vista of hope that is not really tolerable since the sufferer could not endure the disappointment of that hope remaining unfulfilled.

**The Healing Gifts of the Spirit.*

There is also an opposite danger for those who will not face the possibility of failure in a healing enterprise. Somerset Maugham, in his novel *Of Human Bondage* depicts a small boy, Philip, who prays in perfect faith for the removal of the club foot which makes him the object of ridicule at school. The pain of *not* having his prayer answered induces in him a total cynicism about all religious statements, together with a profound distrust in the authority of the Church, which aroused within him such a profound expectation that found no fulfilment.

All healing processes inevitably arouse some degree of hope, and this is a tremendous responsibility which must be handled with extraordinary sensitivity if the last state of many sick people is not going to be worse than the first.

Mrs. Sanford's comment that 'all prayer is in essence an attempt to work out and establish what we believe to be God's will', however, perhaps comes nearer to the creative approach to suffering that is adopted by Burrswood. The Burrswood healing service uses that surrender of the individual will as the pivot on which healing turns. The complexity of illness is such that probably no one except the individual sufferer and God can fully know the whole truth. The illness may be caused by sin — the sin of parents or forebears, the sin of husband or wife, the sin of society, or the patient's sin, or it may be caused by something even more mysterious, the patient's need to suffer, not necessarily for reasons of guilt or masochism, but as part of his growth, part of his self-understanding, and so of his capacity to enter creatively into the suffering of the world. It may be as much of a mystery to him as it is to everyone else, yet he will need to live out the pain and fear and confusion of the mystery within a framework of meaning, though not necessarily of healing in the sense of immediate cure. He may need *care*, the care of those who will listen and pay attention to his struggles, as much as, or more than, he needs cure.

In discussing various approaches to healing we have so far looked at the conventional hospital setting where the emphasis is usually on physical cure, and of the practice of prayer and the laying-on of hands as an exercise working side by side with this, but a crucial area of healing, that of the mind, has so far been left out.

Attempts and methods to cure people through their minds seem to grow daily more numerous. There is the psychiatry practised within conventional medicine, where use is made of drugs, surgery and such techniques as electro-convulsive therapy, rather more than 'talking' methods. There is the psychoanalytical method, deriving from Freud, in which the patient spends many hours with the analyst, associating freely to present and past experiences, forming a relationship with the analyst which Freud called a 'transference', which is itself analysed. Freud saw the analyst as acting like a mirror in which the patient could catch sight of his own unconscious processes, processes which had often in the past brought about pain and failure in relationships or in achievement, and which if undiscovered would do so again.

Another school of analysis is analytical psychology, the Jungian school. Jung, unlike Freud, felt that on the whole the unconscious processes were to be trusted, that they led the human personality which, in immaturity was centred on the ego, into a new wholeness which he called the 'Self'. In our time, however, and particularly in the West, there was a tendency to deny the voice of the unconscious and to limit the personality to the ego, and this led to a deathly sickness, both for the individual and the collective. Religion, which supremely had encouraged men to trust the voice of the unconscious, was losing its force, and in its absence men turned clamorously to ideologies capable of massive destruction. The remedy was a return to listening to the voice of the unconscious as it spoke to men in the symbols of art and religion, in the myths of our ancestors, and in dreams. For individuals entering analysis with Jungian analysts it was also a matter of feeling their way towards self-knowledge by symbols and dreams, and by analysis of the transference and the events of daily life.

Apart from these two major schools of psychoanalysis psychotherapists sprang up deriving their inspiration from neo-Freudians or neo-Jungians. Some practise healing methods that are a combination of both schools. There are also group therapy methods, encounter groups, courses aimed at taking the patient back to the traumatic episodes of infancy ('the primal scream') and many more.

As with all methods of healing there are criticisms of all schools. The hospital use of drugs and mechanical methods seems alarmingly impersonal, and shows scant concern, in many cases, for achieving a real understanding of the patient's problems. In a society where many appear to be sick just because no one pays real attention to them, it is disturbing that even in a state of breakdown or attempted suicide their cry is still not truly listened to. On the other hand, there are temporary conditions of emotional illness and some permanent ones that are immensely eased by such treatments, and in a system with many patients and little money, it may be unrealistic to insist that more is required.

By contrast the private treatment of patients by analysis is very costly indeed, since a patient in full analysis needs to visit the analyst three or four times a week. It is not entirely true that only the rich can afford analysis — there are a handful of clinics available where analysis can be had more cheaply, and many analysts take deserving cases at a reduced fee. However, it tends to be the professional classes who benefit, and it is not altogether easy, since the patient takes up such an enormous amount of the therapist's time, to see how the cost could be reduced.

There is, in any case, much prejudice against these methods, partly because of their length, partly because of the absurdity with which some analysts have practised their art, and partly, probably, because of the deep fear that most people have of introspection. In Christian circles, until recently, there was anxiety that the permissive attitude of the analyst in allowing his patient to speak of his fantasies or perversions without censure, was a sort of condoning of immoral attitudes.

R. Assagioli, an Italian psychologist, borrowing heavily from Jung in his ideas, counters this fear by his emphasis on the will, and by his understanding of personal human development as leading into spiritual understanding — a development he calls 'psychosynthesis'. His work has acquired some enthusiastic followers in Christian circles, yet some may feel that he does not have the depth of Jung's understanding and is too determined to conform to Christian preconceptions.

Other thinkers in this field with interesting things to say are Abraham Maslow who sees that the key to the struggle of each of us is what he calls 'self-actualisation'. If we are prevented from becoming what is in us to become then we fall into sickness and despair. Viktor Frankl, deriving his theory from the traumatic experiences of a Nazi concentration camp, sees a sense of meaning as being crucial to man's survival and wellbeing. Take this from him, as happened to many prisoners in the camps, suddenly plunged into a nightmare existence for which nothing in their previous life had prepared them spiritually, and he is as good as dead. The individual, and indeed whole societies, must search for meaning and live for it.

What is common to all these methods except conventional psychiatry is that they encourage men to look within for the cause of their malaise, and not regard it as a purely fortuitous event for which they have no responsibility and are helpless to avert. In this they follow squarely in the tradition of many primitive communities who believe that health comes from 'getting right' with the environment, and with traditional religion with its emphasis on self-examination, followed by self-knowledge and self-criticism, as a path towards the soul's health. Many of those who take part in analytical procedures report moments they can only describe as 'religious' when dreams, symbols, sudden flashes of insight open upon an eternal world — what Jung describes as the moments 'when the imperishable world irrupted into this transitory one.'

Among those who use 'talking' or 'listening' methods to help others, is the huge, and growing, body of 'counsellors'. Some of these are social workers in fully official capacities, others are amateurs, trained to a certain degree, such as marriage guidance workers, Samaritans, sexual counsellors, etc. Some of these would claim to have a kind of 'first aid' function, being available to clients in the first desperate moments when they need someone to turn to, but ready to seek more professional advice if the problems seem intractable. The depths of self-knowledge which are deemed desirable for the analyst (who has undergone lengthy analysis himself before practising) are not necessary here. Many social workers, however, whether professionally trained or not (and most counselling organisations give their workers a reasonable degree of training) become very experienced in caring for people with problems, and unlike the doctor who is often only presented with the physical expression of an intolerable life situation, the social worker is often shown a wider segment of the client's problem, not simply the mental or physical breakdown, but the financial problems, the family and work pressures, which trigger off illness. Whereas the doctor is principally concerned with sickness, and the analyst with the unconscious causes of sickness, the social worker works at the meeting-point of the two, the everyday conditions in which a man or woman's conflicts occur. Like all the others who care for the sick and unhappy, however, the social worker is also the victim of the problems of our society. Like the doctor he or she suffers from the lack of money expended on the social services, so that overwork, and sometimes lack of adequate training, hampers the effectiveness of the work. Perhaps more seriously the impersonality and lack of neighbourly caring in our society increases the burden. Disturbingly, where, in recent years, social workers have failed to intervene at the right moment in cases of cruelty to children or fatal neglect, there has been a tendency to turn upon them in righteous indignation, accusing them of the sins of the rest of society, expecting them to show the insight and the initiative which should equally have been shown by relatives and friends of the families concerned.

In a different capacity to either the analyst, the counsellor or the social worker, is the priest or minister. Those who approach him have many different kinds of problem, but they sense, however dimly, that their problem has a spiritual context. It isn't *just* that they have an unhappy marriage, a sexual problem, a job that they hate, or a bad conscience; it is that these failures are seen by them as bars to the spiritual development they are seeking. There are still many, despite the strong secular influences of our time, for whome health is inseparable from the claims of the spirit. Organisations such as the Clinical Theology Association started by Dr. Frank Lake which strives both to educate the priest or minister in aspects of emotional disturbance which otherwise might remain outside his ken and to integrate many new insights within a Christian framework are of the greatest value in bridging various disciplines. Other counselling organisations with a Christian base are the Westminster Pastoral Foundation and the Dympna Centre.

The priest's role, is, in most cases, a less active one than that of the social worker, a role of hearing confessions, both formally and informally, giving absolution, both formally and informally, befriending in a way that cuts across barriers of age, class and intelligence, and where it seems right and possible, helping isolated individuals to become part of the community. Some of the skills of the social worker may be of great use to him, and many priests, particularly in youth, are tempted to evade the difficulties and ambiguities of the priest's role and interpret their ministry largely in terms of social work. Yet this is to devalue the immense usefulness of the passive role, the ability not to go forth and wage war on sickness and distress, as the doctor or the political activist rightly do, but to take up the suffering into belief, an achievement only possible from a centre of stillness and prayer.

Jill Tweedie has written of the irreplaceable role played by the Church in the long and painful aftermath of the Aberfan disaster.* The local minister had himself lost a child in the catastrophe, in itself a powerful symbol of where the priest stands in relation to human suffering, and it was around him and around the church buildings that the rebuilding of a shattered community and many stricken families took place. Many skilled social workers also took part in aiding the bereaved, and their abilities were used and appreciated, yet the role of the Church was seen in this case to have a very special value of its own. This may partly have been because in that part of Wales the Church is still an important influence on

**The Guardian*, 14th October 1974.

people's lives, but an equally important aspect mentioned by a number of people interviewed was that they felt the Church had no professional axe to grind, it was about caring, but a caring that people engaged in because it was central to their belief, not because they were paid or because it was part of their job. Perhaps too, though this was not so easily put into words, because in the face of an utter and irretrievable disaster, such as that of Aberfan, the pain is such that only a transcendent faith is really able to speak to it. No belief in progress, in the ameliorating of social conditions, helps in such a situation (though it does in others); only a sense of meaning that transcends our short, and often bitterly painful, life on earth, has anything creative to say at such a moment. And as many clergy, and others, know full well, it is often not a matter of *saying* anything, our words usually being utterly inept and inadequate, but a matter of being, and being with.

There is another area of suffering where the priest seems sometimes to have a unique role to play and that is in the area of sin and of evil. There are immense, and growing, difficulties about using the word 'sin', since we become more and more aware that many things for which we felt individuals were 'to blame' in the past turned out to be the result of pressures, social, moral, or emotional, that made a particular course of action almost inevitable. Thus, the stealing of sheep and other foodstuffs in the nineteenth century which was felt to be both wicked and criminal and was punishable by hanging, seems innocent enough to us, since a man's children might starve if, in hard times, he did not make such an attempt, and those from whom he stole had more than enough to eat. Yet there is no doubt that many who turn to clergy for advice are troubled by a sense of sin, for actions or omissions which they believe to have done harm and to be their own fault. They are not seeking to evade responsibility for their actions but to have their awareness recognised, and this recognition by another can be a profoundly healing experience. Of course, some individuals suffer from a pathological sense of guilt believing that they are at fault when no one else would agree with them. Some people suffer in this way during acute depression, and others under particular forms of stress — bereavement, say, or the suicide of someone close to them. But in these cases the discussion may open the way for a more reasonable way of interpreting events, and will in any case relieve the painful loneliness of guilt. Other forms of help may also be necessary, but many priests exercise a healing function simply by listening to people's account of their moral failures and so releasing the accumulated guilt and shame.

A more difficult question is the confrontation by evil in a direct form — in the matter of witchcraft, poltergeists, devils, etc. Much controversy has been aroused in the last few years about whether the priest should be involved in exorcism ceremonies, or whether, as a Church of Scotland report claimed, such things are all a matter for the doctor and the psychiatrist since they are all manifestations of mental illness. This seems too summary a way to dismiss phenomena experienced by many normal people, and also an abdication of a concern and responsibility which the Church shouldered for centuries. Just because the irrational makes them feel uneasy, rationalists cannot necessarily dismiss it by ignoring it or pretending that it is wholly understood by 'science'. Most doctors would not claim to feel at ease in cases where patients claim to be 'possessed', any more than most priests, nor would putting a name to the condition, such as schizophrenia, necessarily either explain or relieve the suffering. Perhaps Dorothy Kerin's gentle suggestion that the 'possessed' needed to be gradually filled with loving and positive thoughts before 'the demon' could be persuaded to leave, comes nearer to understanding this particular agony.

All these helpers of the sick are only of service if they can enter with some degree of imagination the plight of those who come to them. It is a curious feature of being human that we are able to imagine with great thoroughness, pains, disabilities and fears from which we have never suffered. But to do this we have to have *some* first-hand experience of suffering through which we can interpret the suffering of another, and because of this the skill of the healer is often dependent upon his own wounds, healed or unhealed. Suffering is a mystery, a mystery shot through with darkness and light, with sadness and joy, but one of the joyful parts of the mystery is the way men and women use experiences that initially seemed intolerable, to bring relief and hope to others.

3

Health

WE HAVE LOOKED at sickness and found it full of ambiguities. Is it in the mind, the body, or the spirit? We scarcely know, since sometimes it is evident in one, sometimes in another. Is it to be cured by the surgeon, the physician, the priest, the social worker or the psychotherapist? Does it need surgery, drugs, mechanical aids, the laying-on of hands, prayer, or simply a listening ear? Each and all of these may help particular extremities of human need. Some who bear distressing diseases seem more whole than those who have 'never had a day's illness'. Some who have excellent physical health seem to be scarcely alive to the deeper meanings and complexities of life. Some seem to be ill because of a headlong flight from life and its demands. Others discover themselves, often for the first time, in the dark pathways of suffering and sickness. No one view of sickness is adequate. If we are to begin to penetrate its profound meaning then we have to stretch our minds almost beyond our present endurance, to hold together complexities and contradictions which may fill us with disquiet. We may have to bear 'miracles', but also the most humdrum details of administration, often so crucial to human wellbeing and happiness. We will have to learn that even the most perfect medical system cannot ease some aspects of human suffering which are properly the province of faith, but that faith, if it is to be effective, has to rid itself of wish-fulfilments and credulities which cheapen our understanding of God.

But if this is our approach to sickness, what is our view of health? Is it equally ambiguous, equally compounded of many disparate elements? Michael Wilson* makes the telling point that health is an unselfconscious state — it is only pain or

**Health is for People*, Darton, Longman & Todd.

discomfort which makes us think about the working of our bodies and minds — and it is not easy to imagine how by thinking about it we can become unselfconscious. Wilson thinks that we have mistaken many things for health and lived to reap the tragic consequences — hygiene, having enough of the necessities of life, stamping out serious diseases, removing death and incurable conditions from public view, having better qualified doctors and better equipped hospitals. What these add up to is what he calls a 'sanitised society', and a sanitised society, at least as we have seen it in Britain, does not seem to succeed in bringing about a state of affairs with which everyone is very happy, least of all the doctors who have contributed most to its real achievements. Something is still very wrong.

Wilson's answer is a more paradoxical approach to health, a sort of *Alice Through the Looking-glass* method. 'Health cannot be ensured. Like love and truth "it resents approaches that are too intense." We can only pay attention to the things which make health possible. Health comes as a surprise. The guest, whose room has been prepared, arrives: but unexpectedly. Health is a gift, a grace.' He suggests that health, and our ever more frantic search for it, is really our disguise for the spiritual search which is basic to the life of every man and woman.

> Health has this quality of restlessness. It could be that our search for health is the secular mould in which our search for God is cast. We do not find 'God-talk' meaningful, and 'holiness' is sadly devalued. So we speak of our search in a different language, the language of health. But we are betrayed. For our Western conception of health is hollow. We have discerned death as the enemy, but have mistaken his shape. Natural death is the friend of man. We can but stave off his untimely arrival.
>
> But the death of quality, whose shape is meaninglessness, whose terror is aloneness, and whole sting is dehumanization, we hardly dare to recognise in ourselves. The splendid weapons of medicine and surgery with which we try to keep

death at bay, are inappropriate here. They bring us wellness, and for this our appetite is ravenous though perverted. We are already well enough. We exist long enough.

In the struggle for health — for meaning, for community and for fuller humanity — the tools are different. If health is a gift we need not only to strive but also to listen, to bear, to wait, to wonder and to worship. We are what we receive.

Health does not exist as a present contentment but in our restlessness. We do not ask a child why he is dancing. We dance too. And we live to dance another day faster and more furiously.

Healthy for what? For God. For that which is at the heart of all that is, in which we live and move and have our being. For the ultimate Context.

The experience of health, because it is a foretaste of wholeness to come, contains, like beauty, love and joy, the answer in itself.

Wilson, the doctor, sees our desperate quest for health as the search for God in disguise, and it was this which Dorothy Kerin, coming at the problem of sickness from a different standpoint, also perceived. Some move directly towards God by means of sickness, some struggle for a lifetime with it as part of the process of knowing God, and some, perhaps the most tragic, appear to use it as an escape from God and his demands upon their life. So that any healer, at whatever level he may be working, and there is need for every level from the directly spiritual to the most obscurely so, needs to see in every patient the whole person struggling within the sick body or the distressed mind.

But if it is wholeness we prize then we need to be critical of the values of a society which disintegrates us. We need to be critical on a practical level — of the way institutions (for the old, the permanently handicapped) which offer care rather than cure are the Cinderellas of our society, of dreadful living conditions which destroy family life and affect the development of children, of the fierce competitiveness of our education system, and the unutterable tedium of many of our jobs. Over against these negative criticisms we need a new vision of community which will help to draw the old, the sick, the handicapped, the unhappy back into the world, not as objects of pity, but as people who have gifts to offer. Loneliness, and the depersonalisation which results, is the worst of problems in Western society, seeming to affect the young as much as the old, and to reap a terrible harvest in terms of depression, suicide, alcoholism, and many other human catastrophes.

Hospitals and health centres cannot ignore the extent to which their patients are already damaged by such social pressures and part of their healing function must be to organise themselves in a way that affirms individuals and counteracts the depersonalising pressures. Many people may have useful gifts to offer in helping to bring about this affirmation, and not all of them need medical training. But perhaps even the more conventional types of treatment need to be more broadly based. Wilson suggests that the general practitioner should be a *troika* of nurse, doctor and social worker.

Burrswood, working in a rather special situation, has already pioneered many ideas which could be copied elsewhere. The warmth of reception on arrival, the flowers, pictures, and beautiful objects which decorate the house, the individual charm of the rooms, the time spent talking to people, the care with which food is cooked and served, the loveliness of the gardens, the easy harmony with which doctors, nurses and other members of staff work together for the common good of the patient, all make the place an oasis for people who have come from institutions where they feel (as one remarked) just a number, or from the strains or loneliness of life at home. But more oases are needed, and every hospital could potentially be one. It can be objected that the Burrswood staff are 'dedicated', as indeed they are, yet many men and women still train to be doctors and nurses within the health service who begin with an equal sense of dedication, a sense that is sometimes destroyed by the example and indifference of fellow-workers. Is it, as Wilson says, that we have learned to put 'cure' before 'care' and so destroyed the very basis of healing, where care is always the primary objective?

It seems probable that we shall not recover this sense of care without a renewed sense of the meaning of life and our own dedication to that meaning, and some would doubt, as the Duke of Edinburgh does in the following passage, that such a sense of meaning is really possible without at least a rudimentary religious faith.

> Until it can be demonstrated that science, technology and economic growth can take the place of religion and provide that essential inspiration and motive which has created all great civilizations in the past, it would appear that our culture is simply free-wheeling on our Christian inheritance . . . The very essence of most religions . . . is that they provide the only satisfactory alternative to expediency in making judgements and decisions on the important issues which each generation has to face.

In the end it looks as if, in our search for health we must search for the religious meaning of our lives, either in a direct approach to God in prayer and contemplation, if we feel able to undertake this, or an opening of our hearts and minds to the unconscious processes by such means as art, nature, human love, and some kinds of psychological analyses. Self-realisation and self-knowledge, as well as self-denial, will play a real part in the healing of ourselves and others, bringing the humour, the insight, the first-hand experience, the patience and the endurance which are needed to confront the harsh realities of pain and grief.

In the course of growth we must all of us suffer and the religious attitude is to accept the suffering that comes our way gracefully, saying, with the old rabbi, not "That's bad, that's bad!" but only "That's bitter, that's bitter!" — recognising the medicine that will deepen our humanity, if we will give it the chance. In gifted healers, like Dorothy Kerin, we can perceive the 'wound' which makes them alive to the wounds of all who come to them, acutely sensitive to pain, yet shrewd about the falsities and evasions with which many of us try to dodge the full implications of our humanity.

Even those who are not formally Christian may find in the

death and resurrection of Christ the most profound of metaphors about suffering, recognising that from pain, despair, loneliness and death, faithfully undergone, new life can flow which transforms the world. It is transformation that we seek, in our own lives, and in the lives of our society, and we find it by faithfully following the life of the spirit, by affirming one another in love, and by finding ourselves affirmed in God.